**Warren's Abstract Mac'**

MW00844976

## Logic Programming

Ehud Shapiro, editor

Koichi Furukawa, Jean-Louis Lassez, Fernando Pereira, and David H. D. Warren, associate editors

*The Art of Prolog: Advanced Programming Techniques*, Leon Sterling and Ehud Shapiro, 1986

*Logic Programming: Proceedings of the Fourth International Conference* (volumes 1 and 2), edited by Jean-Louis Lassez, 1987

*Concurrent Prolog: Collected Papers* (volumes 1 and 2), edited by Ehud Shapiro, 1987

*Logic Programming: Proceedings of the Fifth International Conference and Symposium*, (volumes 1 and 2), edited by Robert A. Kowalski and Kenneth A. Bowen, 1988

*Constraint Satisfaction in Logic Programming*, Pascal van Hentenryck, 1989

*Logic-Based Knowledge Representation*, edited by Peter Jackson, Han Reichgelt, and Frank van Harmelen, 1989

*Logic Programming: Proceedings of the Sixth International Conference*, edited by Giorgio Levi and Maurizio Martelli, 1989

*Meta-Programming in Logic Programming*, edited by Harvey Abramson and M. H. Rogers, 1989

*Logic Programming: Proceedings of the North American Conference* (volumes 1 and 2), edited by Ewing L. Lusk and Ross A. Overbeek, 1989

*Logic Programming: Proceedings of the 1990 North American Conference*, edited by Saumya Debray and Manuel Hermenegildo, 1990

*Logic Programming: Proceedings of the Seventh International Conference*, edited by David H. D. Warren and Peter Szeredi, 1990

*The Craft of Prolog*, Richard O'Keefe, 1990

*Eco-Logic: Logic-Based Approaches to Ecological Modelling*, David Robertson, Alan Bundy, Robert Muetzelfeldt, Mandy Haggith, and Michael Uschold, 1991

*Warren's Abstract Machine: A Tutorial Reconstruction*, Hassan Aït-Kaci, 1991

# Warren's Abstract Machine
A Tutorial Reconstruction

Hassan Aït-Kaci

The MIT Press
Cambridge, Massachusetts
London, England

©1991 Massachusetts Institute of Technology

All rights reserved. No part of this book may be reproduced in any form by any electronic or mechanical means (including photocopying, recording, or information storage and retrieval) without permission in writing from the publisher.

This book was set in Computer Modern by the author and printed and bound in the United States of America.

Library of Congress Cataloging-in-Publication Data

Aït-Kaci, Hassan, 1954–
    Warren's abstract machine : a tutorial reconstruction / Hassan Aït-Kaci.
        p.    cm. — (Logic programming)
    Includes bibliographical references and index.
    ISBN 0-262-01123-9 (hc). — ISBN 0-262-51058-8 (pbk.)
    1. Prolog (Computer program language) 2. Logic programming. 3. Electronic digital computers. I. Title. II. Series.
QA76.73.P76A38   1991
006.3—dc20                                                                        91-10776
                                                                                        CIP

Because they have seen it grow from the start,
this modest work is dedicated to:

**Eliès, Jayd, Nassim, and Julieta**

*for much needed love
and trusting me, always*

**Nanie**

*for tranquil unconditional faith
and being there*

**Forêt des Flambertins**

*for peaceful mornings
and conniving whispers
giving me some answers*

# Contents

# List of Figures

# Series Foreword

The logic programming approach to computing investigates the use of logic as a programming language and explores computational models based on controlled deduction.

The field of logic programming has seen a tremendous growth in the last several years, both in depth and in scope. This growth is reflected in the number of articles, journals, theses, books, workshops, and conferences devoted to the subject. The MIT Press series in logic programming was created to accommodate this development and to nurture it. It is dedicated to the publication of high-quality textbooks, monographs, collections, and proceedings in logic programming.

*Ehud Shapiro*
*The Weizmann Institute of Science*
*Rehovot, Israel*

# Foreword

Prolog was conceived in the early 1970s by Alain Colmerauer and his colleagues at the University of Marseille. It was the first practical embodiment of the concept of logic programming, due to Robert Kowalski. The key idea behind logic programming is that computation can be expressed as controlled deduction from declarative statements. Although the field has developed considerably since those early days, Prolog remains the most fundamental and widely used logic programming language.

The first implementation of Prolog was an interpreter written in Fortran by members of Colmerauer's group. Although in some ways quite crude, this implementation was a milestone in several ways: it established the viability of Prolog, it helped to disseminate the language, and it laid the foundations of Prolog implementation technology. A later milestone was perhaps the DEC-10 Prolog system developed at the University of Edinburgh by myself and colleagues. This system built on the Marseille implementation techniques by introducing the notion of compiling Prolog into a low-level language (in this case DEC-10 machine code), as well as various important space-saving measures. I later refined and abstracted the principles of the DEC-10 Prolog implementation into what is now known as the WAM (Warren Abstract Machine).

The WAM is an abstract machine consisting of a memory architecture and instruction set tailored to Prolog. It can be realised efficiently on a wide range of hardware, and serves as a target for portable Prolog compilers. It has now become accepted as a standard basis for implementing Prolog. This is personally gratifying, but somewhat embarrassing in that the WAM is perhaps too readily accepted as the standard. Although the WAM is a distillation of a long line of experience in Prolog implementation, it is by no means the only possible point to consider in the design space. For example, whereas the WAM adopts "structure copying" to represent Prolog terms, the "structure sharing" representation used in the Marseille and DEC-10 implementations still has much to recommend it. Be that as it may, I believe the WAM is certainly a good starting point for studying Prolog implementation technology.

Regrettably, until now, there has not been a good source for getting acquainted with the WAM. My original technical report is not easily accessible, and contains only a "bare bones" definition of the abstract machine, written for an expert reader. Other works have discussed the WAM from various points of view, but there has continued to be a lack of a good tutorial introduction.

It is therefore a great pleasure to see the emergence of this excellent tutorial

by Hassan Aït-Kaci. The book is a delight to read. It explains the WAM
with great clarity and elegance. I believe readers with an interest in computer
science will find this book provides a stimulating introduction to the fascinating
subject of Prolog implementation. I am most grateful to Hassan for making
my work accessible to a wider audience.

*David H. D. Warren*
*Bristol, UK*
*February 1991*

# Acknowledgments

First and foremost, David H. D. Warren is the person to whom I must express not only my awe for having invented and described the WAM, but also my most sincere gratitude for never minding my repeatedly pestering him with questions about minute details he had to dredge out from the deeps of his memory. I am all the more indebted to him as I know how busy he never ceases being, designing better and faster architectures, way ahead of most of us, no longer worrying about this prehistoric part of his research life. In addition, I am particularly flattered that he spontaneously cared to judge this humble opus to be a contribution worth being part of the prestigious MIT Press Logic Programming Series. Finally, let him be again thanked for granting me the honor of introducing it with a foreword.

To be honest, it is rather ironical that I, slow-witted as I notoriously am, be credited with explaining the WAM to the world at large. In truth, my own deciphering of the WAM's intricacies has been a painful and lengthy process. As a matter of fact, I owe my basic understanding of it to two dear friends, specifically. Thus, I would like to thank Roger Nasr for introducing the WAM to me and Manuel Hermenegildo for patiently explaining it to me a hundred times over. They deserve most of the credit bestowed on me as this monograph's author, having given me the foundations upon which I structured my presentation.

This tutorial was, in an earlier version, a technical report of the Digital Equipment Corporation's Paris Research Laboratory (PRL). Several people contributed to improve on the form and contents of that report and thence of this ensuing monograph. Thus, I am very much in debt to Manuel Hermenegildo, David Barker-Plummer, and David H. D. Warren, for the precious favor of proofreading a first draft, making some important corrections. Many thanks are due also to Patrick Baudelaire, Michel Gangnet, Solange Karsenty, Richard Meyer, and Ascánder Suárez, for suggesting several emendations, having gracefully volunteered to plow through the draft.

As the PRL report was being disseminated, I began receiving feedback from attentive readers. Some of them caught a few serious bugs that remained in that report making some material, as presented there, insidiously incorrect. Naturally, all those mistakes have now been corrected in this monograph, and, where appropriate, mention is made of those who brought to my attention my erroneous account. Nevertheless, I would like to express here my gratitude to those who kindly reported bugs, made insightful comments, gave disturbing counter-examples, or proposed better explanations. They are: Christoph

Beierle, André Bolle, Damian Chu, William Clocksin, Maarten van Emden, Michael Hanus, Pascal van Hentenryck, Juhani Jaakola, Stott Parker, Fernando Pereira, Frank Pfenning, Dave Raggett, Dean Rosenzweig, David Russinoff, and two anonymous reviewers. All remaining mistakes are to be blamed on my own incompetence and still imprecise understanding.

Having been presumptuous enough to envisage elaborating the original tutorial into book form, I have benefitted from the kind advice and efficient assistance of Bob Prior, editor at MIT Press. I thank him for everything—his patience in particular.

Finally, I gratefully acknowledge the benevolent agreement kindly given to me by Patrick Baudelaire, director of PRL, and Sam Fuller, Digital's vice-president for Corporate Research and Architecture, to let me publish the work as a book. I am quite obliged for their *laisser-faire*.

*H.A.-K.*
*Rueil-Malmaison, France*
*January 1991*

# Warren's Abstract Machine

Nobody told them what it was. The thing was going very slowly. I said that the first thing there has to be is that these technical guys know what we're doing. ... I could give a nice lecture about what we were doing, and they were all excited ... They understood everything; ... and all that had to be done was to tell them what it was.

RICHARD P. FEYNMAN
*Surely You're Joking, Mr. Feynman*

# 1 Introduction

In 1983, David H. D. Warren designed an abstract machine for the execution of Prolog consisting of a memory architecture and an instruction set [War83]. This design became known as the Warren Abstract Machine (WAM) and has become the *de facto* standard for implementing Prolog compilers. In [War83], Warren describes the WAM in a minimalist's style, making understanding very difficult for the average reader, even with a foreknowledge of Prolog's operations. Too much is left untold, and very little is justified in clear terms.[1] This has resulted in a very scant number of WAM *aficionados* who could boast understanding the details of its workings. Typically, these have been Prolog implementors who decided to invest the necessary time to learn by doing and to reach enlightenment painstakingly.

## 1.1 Existing literature

Witness to this lack of understanding is the fact that in six years there has been little published that would teach the WAM, let alone formally justify its correctness. Indeed, besides Warren's original hermetic report [War83], there has been virtually no official publication on the WAM. A few years ago, one could come across a draft authored by a group at Argonne National Laboratory [GLLO85]. But, to be honest, we found that manuscript even harder to understand than Warren's report. The flaw was that it insisted in presenting the complete WAM as is, rather than as a gradually transformed and optimized design.

A gradual refinement style has in fact been used by David Maier and David S. Warren[2] in [MW88]. There, one can find a description of techniques of Prolog compilation akin to the WAM's.[3] However, we believe that this otherwise quite commendable effort still suffers from a few drawbacks as a definitive tutorial. First, it describes a close variant of the WAM rather than, strictly speaking, the WAM itself. That is, not all of the WAM's features are covered. Moreover, explanations are limited to illustrative examples and seldom make explicitly and exhaustively clear the specific context in which some optimizations apply. Second, the part devoted to compilation

---

[1] David H. D. Warren's confides privately that he "felt [that the WAM] was important, but [its] details unlikely to be of wide interest. Hence, [he used a] 'personal notes' style."

[2] A different person than the WAM's designer, for whose research the WAM has been of great inspiration. In turn, interestingly enough, David H. D. Warren has lately been working on a parallel architecture for Prolog whose abstract model shares its essence with some ideas independently conceived by David S. Warren.

[3] *Op. Cit.*, Chapter 11.

of Prolog comes very late in the book—in the penultimate chapter—relying, for implementation details, on overly detailed Pascal procedures and data structures incrementally refined over the previous chapters. We feel that this sidetracks reading and obfuscates to-the-point learning of the abstract machine. Finally, although it presents a series of gradually refined designs, their tutorial does not separate orthogonal pieces of Prolog in the process. All the versions presented are full Prolog machines. As a result, the reader interested in picking and choosing partial techniques to adapt somewhere else cannot discriminate among these easily. Now, in all fairness, Maier and Warren's book has the different ambition of being a first course in logic programming. Thus, it is actually a feat that its authors were able to cover so much material, both theoretical and practical, and go so far as to include also Prolog compiling techniques. More important, their book is the first available official publication to contain a (real) tutorial on the WAM techniques.

After the preliminary version of this book had been completed, another recent publication containing a tutorial on the WAM was brought to this author's attention. It is a book due to Patrice Boizumault [Boi88] whose Chapter 9 is devoted to explaining the WAM. There again, its author does not use a gradual presentation of partial Prolog machines. Besides, it is written in French—a somewhat restrictive trait as far as its readership is concerned. Still, Boizumault's book is very well conceived, and contains a detailed discussion describing an explicit implementation technique for the *freeze* meta-predicate.[4]

Even more recently, a formal verification of the correctness of a slight simplification of the WAM was carried out by David Russinoff [Rus89]. That work deserves justified praise as it methodically certifies correctness of most of the WAM with respect to Prolog's SLD resolution semantics. However, it is definitely not a tutorial, although Russinoff defines most of the notions he uses in order to keep his work self-contained. In spite of this effort, understanding the details is considerably impeded without working familiarity with the WAM as a prerequisite. At any rate, Russinoff's contribution is nevertheless a *première* as he is the first to establish rigorously something that had been taken for granted thus far. Needless to say, that report is not for the fainthearted.

---

[4]*Op. Cit.*, Chapter 10.

## 1.2   This tutorial

### 1.2.1   Disclaimer and motivation

The length of this monograph has been kept deliberately short. Indeed, this author feels that the typical expected reader of a tutorial on the WAM would wish to get to the heart of the matter quickly and obtain complete but short answers to questions. Also, for reasons pertaining to the specificity of the topic covered, it was purposefully decided not to structure it as a real textbook, with abundant exercises and lengthy comments. Our point is to make the WAM explicit as it was conceived by David H. D. Warren and to justify its workings to the reader with convincing, albeit informal, explanations. The few proposed exercises are meant more as an aid for understanding than as food for further thoughts.

The reader may find, at points, that some design decisions, clearly correct as they may be, appear arbitrarily chosen among potentially many other alternatives, some of which he or she might favor over what is described. Also, one may feel that this or that detail could be "simplified" in some local or global way. Regarding this, we wish to underscore two points: (1) we chose to follow Warren's original design and terminology, describing what he did as faithfully as possible; and, (2) we warn against the casual thinking up of alterations that, although that may appear to be "smarter" from a local standpoint, will generally bear subtle global consequences interfering with other decisions or optimizations made elsewhere in the design. This being said, we did depart in some marginal way from a few original WAM details. However, where our deviations from the original conception are proposed, an explicit mention will be made and a justification given.

Our motivation to be so conservative is simple: our goal is *not* to teach the world how to implement Prolog optimally, *nor* is it to provide a guide to the state of the art on the subject. Indeed, having contributed little to the craft of Prolog implementation, this author claims glaring incompetence for carrying out such a task. Rather, this work's intention is to explain in simpler terms, and justify with informal discussions, David H. D. Warren's abstract machine *specifically* and *exclusively*. Our source is what he describes in [War83, War88]. The expected achievement is merely the long overdue filling of a gap so far existing for whoever may be curious to acquire *basic* knowledge of Prolog implementation techniques, as well as to serve as a spring board for the expert eager to contribute further to this field for which the WAM is, in fact, just the tip of an iceberg. As such, it is hoped that this monograph would constitute an interesting and self-contained complement to basic textbooks for general courses on logic programming, as well as to those on compiler design for more conventional programming languages. As a stand-alone work, it could be a quick reference for the computer professional in need of direct access to WAM concepts.

### 1.2.2   Organization of presentation

Our style of teaching the WAM makes a special effort to consider carefully each feature of the WAM design in isolation by introducing separately and incrementally distinct aspects of Prolog. This allows us to explain as limpidly as possible specific principles proper to each. We then stitch and merge the different patches into larger pieces, introducing independent optimizations one at a time, converging eventually to the complete WAM design as described in [War83] or as overviewed in [War88]. Thus, in Chapter 2, we consider unification alone. Then, we look at flat resolution (that is, Prolog without backtracking) in Chapter 3. Following that, we turn to disjunctive definitions and backtracking in Chapter 4. At that point, we will have a complete, albeit *naïve*, design for pure Prolog. In Chapter 5, this first-cut design will be subjected to a series of transformations aiming at optimizing its performance, the end product of which is the full WAM. We have also prepared an index for quick reference to most critical concepts used in the WAM, something without which no (real) tutorial could possibly be complete.

It is expected that the reader already has a basic understanding of the operational semantics of Prolog—in particular, of unification and backtracking. Nevertheless, to make this work also profitable to readers lacking this background, we have provided a quick summary of the necessary Prolog notions in Appendix A. As for notation, we implicitly use the syntax of so-called Edinburgh Prolog (see, for instance, [CM84]), which we also recall in that appendix. Finally, Appendix B contains a recapitulation of all explicit definitions implementing the full WAM instruction set and its architecture so as to serve as a complete and concise summary.

# 2 Unification—Pure and Simple

Recall that a (first-order) term is either a *variable* (denoted by a capitalized identifier), a *constant* (denoted by an identifier starting with a lower-case letter) or a *structure* of the form $f(t_1, \ldots, t_n)$ where $f$ is a symbol called a *functor* (denoted as a constant), and the $t_i$'s are first-order terms—the term's *subterms*. The number of subterms for a given functor symbol is predetermined and called its *arity*. In order to allow a symbol to be used with possibly different arities, we shall use the explicit notation '$f/n$' when referring to the functor consisting of the symbol $f$ and arity $n$. Hence, two functors are equal if and only if they have the same symbol *and* arity. Letting $n = 0$, a constant is seen as a special case of a structure. Thus, a constant $c$ will be designated as the functor $c/0$.

We consider here $\mathcal{L}_0$, a very simple language indeed. In this language, one can specify only two sorts of entities: a *program* term and a *query* term. Both program and query are first-order terms but not variables. The semantics of $\mathcal{L}_0$ is simply tantamount to computing the most general unifier of the program and the query. As for syntax, $\mathcal{L}_0$ will denote a program as $t$ and a query as $?-t$ where $t$ is a term. The scope of variables is limited to a program (resp., a query) term. Thus, the meaning of a program (resp., a query) is independent of its variables' names. An interpreter for $\mathcal{L}_0$ will dispose of some data representation for terms and use a unification algorithm for its operational semantics. We next describe $\mathcal{M}_0 = \langle \mathcal{D}_0, \mathcal{I}_0 \rangle$, an abstract machine design for $\mathcal{L}_0$ consisting of a data representation $\mathcal{D}_0$ acted upon by a set $\mathcal{I}_0$ of machine instructions.

The idea is quite simple: having defined a program term $p$, one can submit any query $?-q$ and execution either fails if $p$ and $q$ do not unify, or succeeds with a binding of the variables in $q$ obtained by unifying it with $p$.

## 2.1 Term representation

Let us first define an internal representation for terms in $\mathcal{L}_0$. We will use a global block of storage in the form of an addressable *heap* called HEAP which is an array of data cells. A heap cell's address is its index in the array HEAP.

It will be sufficient, in order to represent arbitrary terms in HEAP, to encode variables and *'structures'* of the form $f(@_1, \ldots, @_n)$ where $f/n$ is a functor and the $@_i$'s are references to the heap addresses the $n$ subterms. Thus, there are two sorts of data to be stored in the array HEAP: variables and structures. Explicit *tags*, appearing as part of the format of some heap cells, will be used to discriminate between these two sorts of heap data.

A variable will be identified to a reference pointer and represented using a single heap cell. Thus, we shall speak of *variable cells*. A variable cell will be identified by the tag REF, as denoted as $\langle$ REF , $k$ $\rangle$ where $k$ is a store address; *i.e.*, an index into HEAP. This convenience is meant to facilitate variable binding by establishing a reference to the term the variable is to be bound to. Thus, upon binding a variable, the address part of the REF cell that represents it will be set accordingly. The convention for representing an *unbound* variable is to set the address part of the REF cell to contain its own address. Therefore an unbound variable is a self-referential REF cell.

Structures are non-variable terms. Thus, the heap format used for representing a structure $f(t_1, \ldots, t_n)$ will consist of $n + 2$ heap cells. The first two of these $n + 2$ cells are not necessarily contiguous. In effect, the first of the two acts as a sorted reference pointer to the second, itself used to represent the functor $f/n$. (The reason for this apparently odd indirection is to accommodate structure sharing as will become clear shortly.) The $n$ other cells are destined to contain references to the roots of the $n$ subterms in proper order. More specifically, the first of the $n + 2$ cells representing $f(t_1, \ldots, t_n)$ is formatted as a tagged *structure cell*, denoted as $\langle$ STR , $k$ $\rangle$, containing the tag STR and the address $k$ where (the representation of) the functor $f/n$ is stored. This cell is called a *functor cell* and, quite importantly, it is *always* immediately followed by a sequence of $n$ contiguous cells, one for each subterm $t_i$, respectively. That is, if HEAP $[k]$ = $f/n$ then HEAP $[k + 1]$ will refer to the first subterm $(t_1)$, ... HEAP $[k + n]$ to the $n$-th (and last) subterm $(t_n)$.

For example, a possible heap representation of the term $p(Z, h(Z, W), f(W))$ starts at address 7 in the heap shown in Figure 2.1. Note that only one occurrence of a given variable is represented by an unbound REF cell, whereas its other occurrences are REF cells containing the heap address of the first occurrence. Observe also that, although it is true that the structure cells at addresses 0, 4, and 7 do contiguously precede their respective functor cells, such is not the case for the structure cells at address 10, and 11.

## 2.2  Compiling $\mathcal{L}_0$ queries

According to $\mathcal{L}_0$'s operational semantics, the processing of a query consists of preparing one side of an equation to be solved. Namely, a query term $q$ is translated into a sequence of instructions designed to build an exemplar of $q$

| 0 | STR | 1 |
|---|-----|---|
| 1 | $h/2$ | |
| 2 | REF | 2 |
| 3 | REF | 3 |
| 4 | STR | 5 |
| 5 | $f/1$ | |
| 6 | REF | 3 |
| 7 | STR | 8 |
| 8 | $p/3$ | |
| 9 | REF | 2 |
| 10 | STR | 1 |
| 11 | STR | 5 |

**Figure 2.1**

Heap representation of $p(Z, h(Z, W), f(W))$.

on the heap from $q$'s textual form. Hence, due to the tree structure of a term and multiple occurrences of variables, it is necessary, while processing a part of the term, to save temporarily someplace pieces of terms yet to be processed or a variable that may occur again later in the term. For this purpose, $\mathcal{M}_0$ is endowed with a sufficient number of (variable) *registers* X1, X2, etc., to be used to store heap data temporarily as terms are being built. Thus, the contents of such a register will have the format of a heap cell. These variable registers are allocated to a term on a least available index basis such that (1) register X1 is always allocated to the outermost term, and (2) the same register is allocated to all the occurrences of a given variable. For example, registers are allocated to the variables of the term $p(Z, h(Z, W), f(W))$ as follows:

$$X1 = p(X2, X3, X4)$$
$$X2 = Z$$
$$X3 = h(X2, X5)$$
$$X4 = f(X5)$$
$$X5 = W.$$

This amounts to saying that a term is seen as a flattened conjunctive set of equations of the form $X_i = X$ or $X_i = f(X_{i_1}, \ldots, X_{i_n})$, ($n \geq 0$) where the $X_i$'s are all distinct new variable names. There are two consequences of register allocation: (1) external variable names (such as $Z$ and $W$ in our example) can all be forgotten; and, (2) a query term can then be transformed into its *flattened form*, a sequence of register assignments only of the form $Xi = f(Xi_1, \ldots, Xi_n)$. This form is what is to guide the building of the term's heap representation. Thus, for left-to-right code generation to be well-founded, it is necessary to order a flattened query term so as to ensure that a register name may not be used in the right-hand side of an assignment (*viz.*, as a subterm) before its assignment, if it has one (*viz.*, being the left-hand side). For example, the flattened form of query term $p(Z, h(Z, W), f(W))$ is the sequence $X3 = h(X2, X5)$, $X4 = f(X5)$, $X1 = p(X2, X3, X4)$.

Scanning a flattened query term from left to right, each component of the form $Xi = f(Xi_1, \ldots, Xi_n)$ is tokenized as a sequence $Xi = f/n$, $Xi_1$, ..., $Xi_n$; that is, a register associated with an $n$-ary functor followed by exactly $n$ register names. Therefore, in a stream of such tokens resulting from tokenizing a full flattened term, there are three kinds of items to process:

1. a register associated with a structure functor;
2. a register argument not previously encountered anywhere in the stream;
3. a register argument seen before in the stream.

From this stream, a token-driven heap representation of the term is easy to obtain. To build it, the actions to be taken for each of the three sorts of tokens are, respectively:

1. push a new STR (and adjoining functor) cell onto the heap and copy that cell into the allocated register address;
2. push a new REF cell onto the heap containing its own address, and copy it into the given register;
3. push a new cell onto the heap and copy into it the register's value.

Each of these three actions specifies the effect of respective instructions of the machine $\mathcal{M}_0$ that we note:

1. put_structure $f/n, Xi$
2. set_variable $Xi$
3. set_value $Xi$

respectively.

From the preceding considerations, it has become clear that the heap is implicitly used as a stack for building terms. Namely, term parts being constructed are incrementally piled on *top* of what already exists in the heap.

---

put_structure $f/n, Xi$ ≡   HEAP[H] ← ⟨STR, H + 1⟩;
                               HEAP[H + 1] ← $f/n$;
                               $Xi$ ← HEAP[H];
                               H ← H + 2;

set_variable $Xi$     ≡   HEAP[H] ← ⟨REF, H⟩;
                               $Xi$ ← HEAP[H];
                               H ← H + 1;

set_value $Xi$       ≡   HEAP[H] ← $Xi$;
                               H ← H + 1;

---

**Figure 2.2**
$\mathcal{M}_0$ machine instructions for query terms

Therefore, it is necessary to keep the address of the next free cell in the heap somewhere, precisely as for a stack.[1] Adding to $\mathcal{M}_0$ a global register H containing at all times the next available address on the heap, these three instructions are given explicitly in Figure 2.2.     For example, given that registers are allocated as above, the sequence of instructions to build the query term $p(Z, h(Z, W), f(W))$, is shown in Figure 2.3.

> **Exercise 2.1** Verify that the effect of executing the sequence of instructions shown in Figure 2.3 (starting with H = 0) does indeed yield a correct heap representation for the term $p(Z, h(Z, W), f(W))$—the one shown earlier as Figure 2.1, in fact.

## 2.3   Compiling $\mathcal{L}_0$ programs

Compiling a program term $p$ is just a bit trickier, although not by much. Observe that it assumes that a query $?-q$ will have built a term on the heap and set register X1 to contain its address. Thus, unifying $q$ to $p$ can proceed by following the term structure already present in X1 as long as it matches functor for functor the structure of $p$. The only complication is that when an unbound REF cell is encountered in the query term in the heap, then it is to be bound to a new term that is built on the heap as an exemplar of the corresponding

---

[1] As a matter of fact, in [War83], Warren refers to the heap as the *global stack*.

```
put_structure h/2, X3   %   ?-X3 = h
set_variable X2         %          (Z,
set_variable X5         %                 W),
put_structure f/1, X4   %       X4 = f
set_value X5            %                (W),
put_structure p/3, X1   %       X1 = p
set_value X2            %                (Z,
set_value X3            %                     X3,
set_value X4            %                           X4).
```

**Figure 2.3**
Compiled code for $\mathcal{L}_0$ query ? -$p(Z, h(Z, W), f(W))$.

subterm in $p$. Therefore, an $\mathcal{L}_0$ program functions in two modes: a read mode in which data on the heap is matched against, and a write mode in which a term is built on the heap exactly as is a query term.

As with queries, register allocation precedes translation of the textual form of a program term into a machine instruction sequence. For example, the following registers are allocated to program term $p(f(X), h(Y, f(a)), Y)$:

$X1 = p(X2, X3, X4)$
$X2 = f(X5)$
$X3 = h(X4, X6)$
$X4 = Y$
$X5 = X$
$X6 = f(X7)$
$X7 = a.$

Recall that compiling a query necessitates ordering its flattened form in such a way as to build a term once its subterms have been built. Here, the situation is reversed because query data from the heap are assumed available, even if only in the form of unbound REF cells. Hence, a program term's flattened form follows a top-down order. For example, the program term $p(f(X), h(Y, f(a)), Y)$ is put into the flattened sequence: $X1 = p(X2, X3, X4)$, $X2 = f(X5)$, $X3 = h(X4, X6)$, $X6 = f(X7)$, $X7 = a$.

As with query compiling, the flattened form of a program is tokenized for left-to-right processing and generates three kinds of machine instructions depending on whether is met:

```
get_structure p/3, X1   %   X1 = p
unify_variable X2       %        (X2,
unify_variable X3       %            X3,
unify_variable X4       %                Y),
get_structure f/1, X2   %   X2 = f
unify_variable X5       %        (X),
get_structure h/2, X3   %   X3 = h
unify_value X4          %        (Y,
unify_variable X6       %            X6),
get_structure f/1, X6   %   X6 = f
unify_variable X7       %        (X7),
get_structure a/0, X7   %   X7 = a.
```

**Figure 2.4**
Compiled code for $\mathcal{L}_0$ program $p(f(X), h(Y, f(a)), Y)$.

1. a register associated with a structure functor;
2. a first-seen register argument; or,
3. an already-seen register argument.

These instructions are,

1. get_structure $f/n$, X$i$
2. unify_variable X$i$
3. unify_value X$i$

respectively.

Taking for example the program term $p(f(X), h(Y, f(a)), Y)$, the $\mathcal{M}_0$ machine instructions shown in Figure 2.4 are generated.   Each of the two unify instructions functions in two modes depending on whether a term is to be matched from, or being built on, the heap. For building (write mode), the work to be done is exactly that of the two set query instructions of Figure 2.2. For matching (read mode), these instructions seek to recognize data from the heap as those of the term at corresponding positions, proceeding if successful and failing otherwise. In $\mathcal{L}_0$, failure aborts all further work. In read mode, these instructions set a global register S to contain at all times the heap address of the next subterm to be matched.

Variable binding creates the possibility that reference chains may be formed.

---

**function** *deref*(*a* : *address*) : *address*;
  **begin**
    ⟨ *tag* , *value* ⟩ ← STORE [*a*] ;
    **if** (*tag* = REF) ∧ (*value* ≠ *a*)
      **then return** *deref*(*value*)
      **else return** *a*
  **end** *deref*;

---

**Figure 2.5**
The *deref* operation

Therefore, *dereferencing* is performed by a function *deref* which, when applied to a store address, follows a possible reference chain until it reaches either an unbound REF cell or a non-REF cell, the address of which it returns. The effect of dereferencing is none other than composing variable substitutions. Its definition is given in Figure 2.5. We shall use the generic notation STORE [*a*] to denote the contents of a term data cell at address *a* (whether heap, X register, or any other global structure, yet to be introduced, containing term data cells). We shall use specific area notation (*e.g.*, HEAP [*a*]) whenever we want to emphasize that the address *a* must necessarily lie within that area.

Mode is set by get_structure $f/n$, X*i* as follows: if the dereferenced value of X*i* is an unbound REF cell, then it is bound to a new STR cell pointing to $f/n$ pushed onto the heap and mode is set to write; otherwise, if it is an STR cell pointing to functor $f/n$, then register S is set to the heap address following that functor cell's and mode is set to read. If it is not an STR cell or if the functor is not $f/n$, the program fails. Similarly, in read mode, unify_variable X*i* sets register X*i* to the contents of the heap at address S; in write mode, a new unbound REF cell is pushed on the heap and copied into X*i*. In both modes, S is then incremented by one. As for unify_value X*i*, in read mode, the value of X*i* must be unified with the heap term at address S; in write mode, a new cell is pushed onto the heap and set to the value of register X*i*. Again, in either mode, S is incremented. All three instructions are expressed explicitly in Figure 2.6.

In the definition of get_structure $f/n$, X*i*, we write *bind*(*addr*, H) to effectuate the binding of the heap cell rather than HEAP [*addr*] ← ⟨ REF , H ⟩ for reasons that will become clear later. The *bind* operation is performed on

---

get_structure $f/n$, X$i$ ≡  *addr* ← *deref*(X$i$);
                     **case** STORE [*addr*] **of**
                            ⟨ REF , _ ⟩ :  HEAP [H] ← ⟨ STR , H + 1 ⟩;
                                          HEAP [H + 1] ← $f/n$;
                                          *bind*(*addr*, H);
                                          H ← H + 2;
                                          *mode* ← write;
                            ⟨ STR , $a$ ⟩ :  **if** HEAP [$a$] = $f/n$
                                          **then**
                                            **begin**
                                                S ← $a$ + 1;
                                                *mode* ← read
                                            **end**
                                            **else** *fail* ← **true**;
                         **other**     :  *fail* ← **true**;
                     **endcase**;

unify_variable X$i$   ≡ **case** *mode* **of**
                         read   :  X$i$ ← HEAP [S];
                         write :  HEAP [H] ← ⟨ REF , H ⟩;
                                       X$i$ ← HEAP [H];
                                       H ← H + 1;
                     **endcase**;
                     S ← S + 1;

unify_value X$i$     ≡ **case** *mode* **of**
                         read   :  *unify*(X$i$, S);
                         write :  HEAP [H] ← X$i$;
                                       H ← H + 1;
                     **endcase**;
                     S ← S + 1;

---

**Figure 2.6**
$\mathcal{M}_0$ machine instructions for programs

two store addresses, at least one of which is that of an unbound REF cell. Its effect, for now, is to bind the unbound one to the other—*i.e.*, change the data field of the unbound REF cell to contain the address of the other cell. In the case where both are unbound, the binding direction is chosen arbitrarily. Later, this will change as a correctness-preserving measure in order to accommodate an optimization. Also, we will see that *bind* is the logical place, when backtracking needs to be considered, for recording effects to be undone upon failure (see Chapter 4, and appendix Section B.2 on Page 101). If wished, *bind* may also be made to perform the *occurs-check* test in order to prevent formation of cyclic terms (by failing at that point). However, the occurs-check test is omitted in most actual Prolog implementations in order not to impede performance.

We must also explicate the *unify* operation used in the matching phase (in read mode). It is a unification algorithm based on the UNION/FIND method [AHU74], where variable substitutions are built, applied, and composed through *dereference* pointers. In $\mathcal{M}_0$ (and in all later machines that will be considered here), this unification operation is performed on a pair of store addresses. It uses a global dynamic structure, an array of store addresses, as a unification stack (called PDL, for Push-Down List). The unification operation is defined as shown in Figure 2.7, where *empty*, *push*, and *pop* are the expected stack operations.

**Exercise 2.2** Give heap representations for the terms $f(X, g(X, a))$ and $f(b, Y)$. Let $a_1$ and $a_2$ be their respective heap addresses, and let $a_X$ and $a_Y$ be the heap addresses corresponding to variables $X$ and $Y$, respectively. Trace the effects of executing *unify*$(a_1, a_2)$, verifying that it terminates with the eventual dereferenced bindings from $a_X$ and $a_Y$ corresponding to $X = b$ and $Y = g(b, a)$.

**Exercise 2.3** Verify that the effect of executing the sequence of instructions shown in Figure 2.4 right after that in Figure 2.3 produces the MGU of the terms $p(Z, h(Z, W), f(W))$ and $p(f(X), h(Y, f(a)), Y)$. That is, the (dereferenced) bindings corresponding to $W = f(a)$, $X = f(a)$, $Y = f(f(a))$, $Z = f(f(a))$.

**Exercise 2.4** What are the respective sequences of $\mathcal{M}_0$ instructions for $\mathcal{L}_0$ *query* term ?-$p(f(X), h(Y, f(a)), Y)$ and *program* term $p(Z, h(Z, W), f(W))$?

**Exercise 2.5** After doing Exercise 2.4, verify that the effect of executing the sequence you produced yields the same solution as that of Exercise 2.3.

---

**procedure** *unify*($a_1, a_2$ : *address*);
  *push*($a_1$, PDL); *push*($a_2$, PDL);
  *fail* ← **false**;
  **while** ¬(*empty*(PDL) ∨ *fail*) **do**
    **begin**
      $d_1$ ← *deref*(*pop*(PDL)); $d_2$ ← *deref*(*pop*(PDL));
      **if** $d_1 \neq d_2$ **then**
        **begin**
          $\langle t_1, v_1 \rangle$ ← STORE[$d_1$]; $\langle t_2, v_2 \rangle$ ← STORE[$d_2$];
          **if** ($t_1$ = REF) ∨ ($t_2$ = REF)
            **then** *bind*($d_1, d_2$)
          **else**
            **begin**
              $f_1/n_1$ ← STORE[$v_1$]; $f_2/n_2$ ← STORE[$v_2$];
              **if** ($f_1$ = $f_2$) ∧ ($n_1$ = $n_2$)
                **then**
                  **for** $i$ ← 1 **to** $n_1$ **do**
                    **begin**
                      *push*($v_1 + i$, PDL);
                      *push*($v_2 + i$, PDL)
                    **end**
                **else** *fail* ← **true**
            **end**
        **end**
      **end**
  **end** *unify*;

---

**Figure 2.7**
The *unify* operation

## 2.4    Argument registers

Since we have in mind to use unification in Prolog for procedure invocation, we can introduce a distinction between atoms (terms whose functor is a predicate) and terms (arguments to a predicate). We thus extend $\mathcal{L}_0$ into a language $\mathcal{L}_1$ similar to $\mathcal{L}_0$ but where a program may be a set of first-order atoms each defining at most one *fact* per predicate name. Thus, in the context of such a program, execution of a query connects to the appropriate definition to use for solving a given unification equation, or fails if none exists for the predicate invoked.

The set of instructions $\mathcal{I}_1$ contains all those in $\mathcal{I}_0$. In $\mathcal{M}_1$, compiled code is stored in a *code area* (CODE), an addressable array of data words, each containing a possibly labeled instruction over one or more memory words consisting of an opcode followed by operands. For convenience, the size of an instruction stored at address $a$ (*i.e.*, CODE[$a$]) will be assumed given by the expression *instruction_size*($a$). Labels are symbolic entry points into the code area that may be used as operands of instructions for transferring control to the code labeled accordingly. Therefore, there is no need to store a procedure name in the heap as it denotes a key into a compiled instruction sequence. Thus, a new instruction call $p/n$ can be used to pass control over to the instruction labeled with $p/n$, or fail if none such exists.

A global register P is always set to contain the address of the next instruction to execute (an instruction counter). The standard execution order of instructions is sequential. Unless failure occurs, most machine instructions (like all those seen before) are implicitly assumed, to increment P by an appropriate offset in the code area as an ultimate action. This offset is the size of the instruction at address P. However, some instructions have for purpose to break the sequential order of execution or to connect to some other instruction at the end of a sequence. These instructions are called *control instructions* as they typically set P in a non-standard way. This is the case of call $p/n$, whose explicit effect, in the machine $\mathcal{M}_1$, is:

$$\text{call } p/n \equiv \text{ P} \leftarrow @(p/n);$$

where the notation $@(p/n)$ stands for the address in the code area of instruction labeled $p/n$. If the procedure $p/n$ is not defined (*i.e.*, if that address is not allocated in the code area), a unification failure occurs and overall execution aborts.

We also introduce another control instruction, proceed, which indicates the end of a fact's instruction sequence. These two new control instructions' effects are trivial for now, and they will be elaborated later. For our present purposes, it is sufficient that proceed be construed as a no-op (*i.e.*, just a code terminator), and call $p/n$ as an unconditional "jump" to the start address of the instruction sequence for program term with functor $p/n$.

Having eliminated predicate symbols from the heap, the unification problem between fact and query terms amounts to solving, not one, but many equations, simultaneously. Namely, there are as many term roots in a given fact or query as there are arguments to the corresponding predicate. Therefore, we must organize registers quite specifically so as to reflect this situation. As we privileged X1 before to denote the (single) term root, we generalize the convention to registers X1 to X$n$ which will now always refer to the first to $n$-th arguments of a fact or query atom. In other words, registers X1, ..., X$n$ are systematically allocated to term roots of an $n$-ary predicate's arguments. To emphasize this, we use a conspicuous notation, writing a register A$i$ rather than X$i$ when it is being used as an argument of an atom. In that case, we refer to that register as an *argument* register. Otherwise, where register X$i$ is not used as an argument register, it is written X$i$, as usual. Note that this is just notation as the A$i$'s are not new registers but the same old X$i$'s used thus far. For example, registers are now allocated for the variables of the atom $p(Z, h(Z, W), f(W))$ as follows:

A1 = $Z$
A2 = $h$(A1, X4)
A3 = $f$(X4)
X4 = $W$.

Observe also that a new situation arises now as variables can be arguments and thus must be handled as roots. Therefore, provision must be made for variables to be loaded into, or extracted from, argument registers for queries and facts, respectively. As before, the necessary instructions correspond to when a variable argument is a first or later occurrence, either in a query or a fact. In a query,

1. the first occurrence of a variable in $i$-th argument position pushes a new unbound REF cell onto the heap and copies it into that variable's register as well as argument register A$i$; and,
2. a later occurrence copies its value into argument register A$i$. Whereas, in a fact,

---

```
put_variable Xn, Ai ≡  HEAP[H] ← ⟨REF, H⟩;
                        Xn ← HEAP[H];
                        Ai ← HEAP[H];
                        H ← H + 1;

put_value Xn, Ai    ≡  Ai ← Xn

get_variable Xn, Ai ≡  Xn ← Ai

get_value Xn, Ai    ≡  unify(Xn, Ai)
```

---

**Figure 2.8**
$\mathcal{M}_1$ instructions for variable arguments

3. the first occurrence of a variable in $i$-th argument position sets it to the value of argument register $Ai$; and,
4. a later occurrence unifies it with the value of $Ai$.

The corresponding instructions are, respectively:

1. `put_variable Xn, Ai`
2. `put_value Xn, Ai`
3. `get_variable Xn, Ai`
4. `get_value Xn, Ai`

and are given explicitly in Figure 2.8.    For example, Figure 2.9 shows code generated for query $?\!-\ p(Z, h(Z, W), f(W))$., and Figure 2.10 that for fact $p(f(X), h(Y, f(a)), Y)$.

> **Exercise 2.6** Verify that the effect of executing the sequence of $\mathcal{M}_1$ instructions shown in Figure 2.9 produces the same heap representation as that produced by the $\mathcal{M}_0$ code of Figure 2.3 (see Exercise 2.1).

> **Exercise 2.7** Verify that the effect of executing the sequence of $\mathcal{M}_1$ instructions shown in Figure 2.10 right after that in Figure 2.9 produces the MGU of the terms $p(Z, h(Z, W), f(W))$ and $p(f(X), h(Y, f(a)), Y)$. That is, the binding $W = f(a), X = f(a), Y = f(f(a)), Z = f(f(a))$.

> **Exercise 2.8** What are the respective sequences of $\mathcal{M}_1$ instructions for $\mathcal{L}_1$ *query* term $?\!-p(f(X), h(Y, f(a)), Y)$ and $\mathcal{L}_1$ *program* term $p(Z, h(Z, W), f(W))$?

```
put_variable X4, A1      %   ?-p(Z,
put_structure h/2, A2    %        h
set_value X4             %         (Z,
set_variable X5          %              W),
put_structure f/1, A3    %                  f
set_value X5             %                     (W)
call p/3                 %                        ).
```

**Figure 2.9**
Argument registers for $\mathcal{L}_1$ query $?-p(Z, h(Z, W), f(W))$.

```
p/3  :   get_structure f/1, A1    %   p(f
         unify_variable X4        %      (X),
         get_structure h/2, A2    %         h
         unify_variable X5        %           (Y,
         unify_variable X6        %               X6),
         get_value X5, A3         %                    Y),
         get_structure f/1, X6    %   X6 = f
         unify_variable X7        %          (X7),
         get_structure a/0, X7    %   X7 = a
         proceed                  %   .
```

**Figure 2.10**
Argument registers for $\mathcal{L}_1$ fact $p(f(X), h(Y, f(a)), Y)$.

**Exercise 2.9**  After doing Exercise 2.8, verify that the effect of executing the sequence you produced yields the same solution as that of Exercise 2.7.

# 3 Flat Resolution

We now extend the language $\mathcal{L}_1$ into a language $\mathcal{L}_2$ where procedures are no longer reduced only to facts but may also have bodies. A body defines a procedure as a conjunctive sequence of atoms. Said otherwise, $\mathcal{L}_2$ is Prolog without backtracking.

An $\mathcal{L}_2$ *program* is a set of procedure definitions or (definite) *clauses*, at most one per predicate name, of the form '$a_0$ : - $a_1, \ldots, a_n$.' where $n \geq 0$ and the $a_i$'s are atoms. As before, when $n = 0$, the clause is called a *fact* and written without the ' : -' implication symbol. When $n > 0$, the clause is called a *rule*, the atom $a_0$ is called its *head*, the sequence of atoms $a_1, \ldots, a_n$ is called its *body* and atoms composing this body are called *goals*. A rule with exactly one body goal is called a *chain* (rule). Other rules are called *deep* rules. $\mathcal{L}_2$ queries are sequences of goals, of the form '? - $g_1, \ldots, g_k$.' where $k \geq 0$. When $k = 0$, the query is called the *empty* query. As in Prolog, the scope of variables is limited to the clause or query in which they appear.

Executing a query '? - $g_1, \ldots, g_k$.' in the context of a program made up of a set of procedure-defining clauses consists of repeated application of *leftmost resolution* until the empty query, or failure, is obtained. Leftmost resolution amounts to unifying the goal $g_1$ with its definition's head (or failing if none exists) and, if this succeeds, executing the query resulting from replacing $g_1$ by its definition body, variables in scope bearing the binding side-effects of unification. Thus, executing a query in $\mathcal{L}_2$ either terminates with success (*i.e.*, it simplifies into the empty query), or terminates with failure, or never terminates. The "result" of an $\mathcal{L}_2$ query whose execution terminates with success is the (dereferenced) binding of its original variables after termination.

Note that a clause with a non-empty body can be viewed in fact as a *conditional* query. That is, it behaves as a query provided that its head successfully unifies with a predicate definition. Facts merely verify this condition, adding nothing new to the query but a contingent binding constraint. Thus, as a first approximation, since an $\mathcal{L}_2$ query (resp., clause body) is a conjunctive sequence of atoms interpreted as procedure calls with unification as argument passing, instructions for it may simply be the concatenation of the compiled code of each goal as an $\mathcal{L}_1$ query making it up. As for a clause head, since the semantics requires that it retrieves arguments by unification as did facts in $\mathcal{L}_1$, instructions for $\mathcal{L}_1$'s fact unification are clearly sufficient.

Therefore, $\mathcal{M}_1$ unification instructions can be used for $\mathcal{L}_2$ clauses, but with two measures of caution: one concerning continuation of execution of a goal sequence, and one meant to avoid conflicting use of argument registers.

## 3.1 Facts

Let us first only consider $\mathcal{L}_2$ facts. Note that $\mathcal{L}_1$ is all contained in $\mathcal{L}_2$. Therefore, it is natural to expect that the exact same compilation scheme for facts carries over untouched from $\mathcal{L}_1$ to $\mathcal{L}_2$. This is true up to a wee detail regarding the `proceed` instruction. It must be made to continue execution, after successfully returning from a call to a fact, back to the instruction in the goal sequence following the call. To do this correctly, we will use another global register CP, along with P, set to contain the address (in the code area) of the next instruction to follow up with upon successful return from a call (*i.e.*, set to P + *instruction_size*(P) at procedure call time). Then, having exited the called procedure's code sequence, execution could thus be resumed as indicated by CP. Thus, for $\mathcal{L}_2$'s facts, we need to alter the effect of $\mathcal{M}_1$'s call $p/n$ to:

call $p/n \equiv$ CP $\leftarrow$ P + *instruction_size*(P);
$\qquad\qquad\qquad$ P $\leftarrow$ @($p/n$);

and that of `proceed` to:

proceed $\equiv$ P $\leftarrow$ CP;

As before, when the procedure $p/n$ is not defined, execution fails.

In summary, with the simple foregoing adjustment, $\mathcal{L}_2$ facts are translated exactly as were $\mathcal{L}_1$ facts.

## 3.2 Rules and queries

We now must think about translating rules. A query is a particular case of a rule in the sense that it is one with no head. It is translated exactly the same way, but without the instructions for the missing head. The idea is to use $\mathcal{L}_1$'s instructions, treating the head as a fact, and each goal in the body as an $\mathcal{L}_1$ query term in sequence; that is, roughly translate a rule '$p_0(\dots)$ :- $p_1(\dots),\dots,p_n(\dots)$.' following the pattern:

*get arguments of* $p_0$
*put arguments of* $p_1$
call $p_1$

$\qquad \vdots$

*put arguments of* $p_n$
call $p_n$

Here, in addition to ensuring correct continuation of execution, we must arrange for correct use of argument registers. Indeed, since the same registers are used by each goal in a query or body sequence to pass its arguments to the procedure it invokes, variables that occur in many different goals in the scope of the sequence need to be protected from the side effects of put instructions. For example, consider the rule '$p(X, Y)$ :- $q(X, Z), r(Z, Y)$.' If the variables $Y, Z$ were allowed to be accessible only from an argument register, no guarantee could be made that they still would be after performing the unifications required in executing the body of $p$.

Therefore, it is necessary that variables of this kind be saved in an *environment* associated with each activation of the procedure they appear in. Variables which occur in more than one body goal are dubbed *permanent* as they have to outlive the procedure call where they first appear. All other variables in a scope that are not permanent are called *temporary*. We shall denote a permanent variable as Y$i$, and use X$i$ as before for temporary variables. To determine whether a variable is permanent or temporary in a rule, the head atom is considered to be part of the first body goal. This is because get and unify instructions do not load registers for further processing. Thus, the variable $X$ in the example above is temporary as it does not occur in more than one goal in the body (*i.e.*, it is not affected by more than one goal's put instructions).

Clearly, permanent variables behave like conventional local variables in a procedure. The situation is therefore quite familiar. As is customary in programming languages, we protect a procedure's local variables by maintaining a run-time stack of procedure activation frames in which to save information needed for the correct execution of what remains to be done after returning from a procedure call. We call such a frame an *environment frame*. We will keep the address of the latest environment on top of the stack in a global register E.[1]

As for continuation of execution, the situation for rules is not as simple as that for facts. Indeed, since a rule serves to invoke further procedures in its body, the value of the program continuation register CP, which was saved at the point of its call, will be overwritten. Therefore, it is necessary to preserve continuation information by saving the value of CP along with permanent variables.

---

[1] In [War83], this stack is called the *local stack* to distinguish it from the global stack (see Footnote 1 at the bottom of Page 9).

Let us recapitulate: $\mathcal{M}_2$ is an augmentation of $\mathcal{M}_1$ with the addition of a new data area, along with the *heap* (HEAP), the *code area* (CODE), and the *push-down list* (PDL). It is called the *stack* (STACK) and will contain procedure activation frames. Stack frames are called *environments*. An environment is pushed onto STACK upon a (non-fact) procedure entry call, and popped from STACK upon return. Thus, an allocate/deallocate pair of instructions must bracket the code generated for a rule in order to create and discard, respectively, such environment frames on the stack. In addition, deallocate being the ultimate instruction of the rule, it must connect to the appropriate next instruction as indicated by the continuation pointer that had been saved upon entry in the environment being discarded.

Since the size of an environment varies with each procedure in function of its number of permanent variables, the stack is organized as a linked list through a *continuation environment* slot; *i.e.*, a cell in each environment frame bearing the stack index of the environment previously pushed onto the stack.

To sum up, two new $\mathcal{I}_2$ instructions for $\mathcal{M}_2$ are added to the ones we defined for $\mathcal{I}_1$:

1. allocate
2. deallocate

with effect, respectively:

1. to allocate a new environment on the stack, setting its continuation environment field to the current value of E, and its continuation point field to that of CP; and,
2. to remove the environment frame at stack location E from the stack and proceed, resetting P to the value of its CP field and E to the value of its CE field.

To have proper effect, an allocate instruction needs to have access to the size of the current environment in order to increment the value of E by the right stack offset. The necessary piece of information is a function of the calling clause (*i.e.*, the number of permanent variables occurring in the calling clause). Therefore, it is easily statically available at the time the code for the calling clause is generated. Now, the problem is to transmit this information to the called procedure that, if defined as a rule (*i.e.*, starting with an allocate), will need it dynamically, depending on which clause calls it. A simple solution is to save this offset in the calling clause's environment frame from where it can be retrieved by a callee that needs it. Hence, in $\mathcal{M}_2$, an additional slot in an environment is set by `allocate` to contain the number of permanent variables in the clause in question.

Summing up again, an $\mathcal{M}_2$ stack environment frame contains:

1. the address in the code area of the next instruction to execute upon (successful) return from the invoked procedure;
2. the stack address of the previous environment to reinstate upon return (*i.e.*, where to pop the stack to);
3. the offset of this frame on the stack (the number of permanent variables); and,
4. as many cells as there are permanent variables in the body of the invoked procedure (possibly none).

Such an $\mathcal{M}_2$ environment frame pushed on top of the stack looks thus:

| | | |
|---:|---|---|
| E | CE | *(continuation environment)* |
| E + 1 | CP | *(continuation point)* |
| E + 2 | $n$ | *(number of permanent variables)* |
| E + 3 | Y1 | *(permanent variable 1)* |
| | $\vdots$ | |
| E + $n$ + 2 | Yn | *(permanent variable n)* |

This necessitates giving `allocate` an explicit argument that is the number of permanent variables of the rule at hand, such that, in $\mathcal{M}_2$:

$$
\begin{aligned}
\text{allocate } N \equiv \quad & newE \leftarrow \text{E} + \text{STACK}[\text{E}+2] + 3; \\
& \text{STACK}[newE] \leftarrow \text{E}; \\
& \text{STACK}[newE+1] \leftarrow \text{CP}; \\
& \text{STACK}[newE+2] \leftarrow N; \\
& \text{E} \leftarrow newE; \\
& \text{P} \leftarrow \text{P} + instruction\_size(\text{P});
\end{aligned}
$$

Similarly, the explicit definition of $\mathcal{M}_2$'s `deallocate` is:

$$
\begin{aligned}
\text{deallocate} \equiv \quad & \text{P} \leftarrow \text{STACK}[\text{E}+1]; \\
& \text{E} \leftarrow \text{STACK}[\text{E}];
\end{aligned}
$$

With this being set up, the general translation scheme into $\mathcal{M}_2$ instructions for an $\mathcal{L}_2$ rule '$p_0(\ldots)$ :- $p_1(\ldots),\ldots,p_n(\ldots)$.' with $N$ permanent variables will follow the pattern:

---

$p/2$ :  `allocate 2`              % $p$
         `get_variable X3, A1`     % $(X,$
         `get_variable Y1, A2`     %    $Y)$ :-
         `put_value X3, A1`        %             $q(X,$
         `put_variable Y2, A2`     %                 $Z$
         `call q/2`                %                   $),$
         `put_value Y2, A1`        %             $r(Z,$
         `put_value Y1, A2`        %                 $Y$
         `call r/2`                %                   $)$
         `deallocate`             %                     $.$

---

**Figure 3.1**
$\mathcal{M}_2$ machine code for rule $p(X, Y)$ :- $q(X, Z), r(Z, Y)$.

$p_0$ :  `allocate` $N$
         *get arguments of* $p_0$
         *put arguments of* $p_1$
         `call` $p_1$
         $\vdots$
         *put arguments of* $p_n$
         `call` $p_n$
         `deallocate`

For example, for $\mathcal{L}_2$ clause '$p(X, Y)$ :- $q(X, Z), r(Z, Y)$.', the corresponding $\mathcal{M}_2$ code is shown in Figure 3.1.

**Exercise 3.1** Give $\mathcal{M}_2$ code for $\mathcal{L}_2$ facts $q(a, b)$ and $r(b, c)$ and $\mathcal{L}_2$ query ?-$p(U, V)$, then trace the code shown in Figure 3.1 and verify that the solution produced is $U = a, V = c$.

# 4 Prolog

The language $\mathcal{L}_3$ (resp., the machine $\mathcal{M}_3$) corresponds to pure Prolog, as it extends the language $\mathcal{L}_2$ (resp., the machine $\mathcal{M}_2$) to allow disjunctive definitions. As in $\mathcal{L}_2$, an $\mathcal{L}_3$ program is a set of procedure definitions. In $\mathcal{L}_3$, a definition is an ordered sequence of clauses (*i.e.*, a sequence of facts or rules) consisting of all and only those whose head atoms share the same predicate name. That name is the name of the procedure specified by the definition. $\mathcal{L}_3$ queries are the same as those of $\mathcal{L}_2$. The semantics of $\mathcal{L}_3$ operates using top-down leftmost resolution, an approximation of SLD resolution. Thus, in $\mathcal{L}_3$, a failure of unification no longer yields irrevocable abortion of execution but considers alternative choices of clauses in the order in which they appear in definitions. This is done by chronological backtracking; *i.e.*, the latest choice at the moment of failure is reexamined first.

It is necessary to alter $\mathcal{M}_2$'s design so as to save the state of computation at each procedure call offering alternatives to restore upon backtracking to this point of choice. We call such a state a *choice point*. We thus need to analyze what information must be saved as a choice point in order to create a record (a choice point frame) wherefrom a correct state of computation can be restored to offer another alternative, with all effects of the failed computation undone. Note that choice point frames must be organized as a stack (just like environments) in order to reflect the compounding of alternatives as each choice point spawns potentially more alternatives to try in sequence.

To distinguish the two stacks, let us call the environment stack the *AND-stack* and the choice point stack the *OR-stack*. As with the AND-stack, we organize the OR-stack as a linked list. The head of this list always corresponds to the latest choice point, and will be kept in a new global register B, such that upon failure, computation is made to resume from the state recovered from the choice point frame indicated by B. When the latest frame offers no more alternatives, it is popped off the OR-stack by resetting B to its predecessor if one exists, otherwise computation fails terminally.

Clearly, if a definition contains only one clause, there is no need to create a choice point frame, exactly as was the case in $\mathcal{M}_2$. For definitions with more than one alternative, a choice point frame is created by the first alternative; then, it is updated (as far as which alternative to try next) by intermediate (but non ultimate) alternatives; finally, it is discarded by the last alternative.

## 4.1 Environment protection

Before we go into the details of what exactly constitutes a choice frame, we must ponder carefully the interaction between the AND-stack and the OR-stack. As long as we considered (deterministic) $\mathcal{L}_2$ program definitions, it was clearly safe to deallocate an environment frame allocated to a rule after successfully falling off the end of the rule. Now, the situation is not quite so straightforward as later failure may force reconsidering a choice from a computation state in the middle of a rule whose environment has long been deallocated. This case is illustrated by the following example program:

$a \; :- \; b(X), c(X).$

$b(X) \; :- \; e(X).$

$c(1).$

$e(X) \; :- \; f(X).$
$e(X) \; :- \; g(X).$

$f(2).$

$g(1).$

Executing '$?-a.$' allocates an environment for $a$, then calls $b$. Next, an environment for $b$ is allocated, and $e$ is called. This creates a choice point on the OR-stack, and an environment for $e$ is pushed onto the AND-stack. At this point the two stacks look thus:[1]

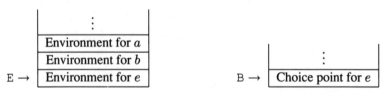

The following call to $f$ succeeds binding $X$ to 2. The environment for $e$ is deallocated, then the environment for $b$ is also deallocated. This leads to stacks looking thus:

---

[1]In these diagrams, the stacks grow downwards; *i.e.*, the stack top is the lower part.

Next, the continuation follows up with execution of $a$'s body, calling $c$, which immediately hits failure. The choice point indicated by B shows an alternative clause for $e$, but at this point *b's environment has been lost.* Indeed, in a more involved example where $c$ proceeded deeper before failing, the old stack space for $b$'s environment would have been overwritten by further calls in $c$'s body.

Therefore, to avoid this kind of misfortune, a setup must be found to prevent unrecoverable deallocation of environment frames whose creation chronologically precedes that of any existing choice point. The idea is that every choice point must "protect" from deallocation all environment frames already existing before its creation. Now, since a stack reflects chronological order, it makes sense to use the same stack for *both* environments and choice points. A choice point now caps all older environments. In effect, as long as it is active, it forces allocation of further environments on top of it, preventing the older environments' stack space to be overwritten even though they may explicitly be deallocated. This allows their safe resurrection if needed by coming back to an alternative from this choice point. Moreover, this "protection" lasts just as long as it is needed since as soon as the choice point disappears, all explicitly deallocated environments can be safely overwritten.

Hence, there is no need to distinguish between the AND-stack from the OR-stack, calling the single one *the* stack. Choice point frames are stored in the stack along with environments, and thus B's value is an address in the stack.

Going back to our example above, the snapshot of the single stack at the same first instant looks thus:

|                | ⋮                     |
|----------------|-----------------------|
|                | Environment for $a$   |
|                | Environment for $b$   |
| B →            | Choice point for $e$  |
| E →            | Environment for $e$   |

and at the same second instant as before, the stack is such that having pushed on it the choice point for $e$ protects $b$'s deallocated environment (which may still be needed by future alternatives given by $e$'s choice point), looking thus:

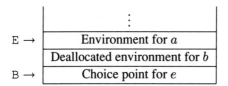

Now, the computation can safely recover the state from the choice point for $e$ indicated by B, in which the saved environment to restore is the one current at the time of this choice point's creation—*i.e.*, that (still existing) of $b$. Having no more alternative for $e$ after the second one, this choice point is discarded upon backtracking, (safely) ending the protection. Execution of the last alternative for $e$ proceeds with a stack looking thus:

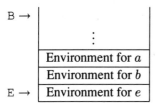

## 4.2   What's in a choice point

When a chosen clause is attempted among those of a definition, it will create side effects on the stack and the heap by binding variables residing there. These effects must be undone when reconsidering the choice. A record must be kept of those variables which need to be reset to 'unbound' upon backtracking. Hence, we provide, along with the heap, the stack, the code area, and the PDL, a new (and last!) data area called the *trail* (TRAIL). This trail is organized as an array of addresses of those (stack or heap) variables which must be reset to 'unbound' upon backtracking. Note that it also works as a stack, and we need a new global register TR always set to contain the top of the trail.

It is important to remark that not all bindings need to be remembered in the trail. Only *conditional* bindings do. A conditional binding is one affecting a variable existing before creation of the current choice point. To determine this, we will use a new global register HB set to contain the value of H at the time of the latest choice point.[2] Hence only bindings of heap (resp., stack) variables whose addresses are *less* than HB (resp., B) need be recorded in the trail. We

---

[2]Strictly speaking, register HB can in fact be dispensed with since, as we see next, its value is that of H which will have been saved in the latest choice point frame.

shall write *trail(a)* when that this operation is performed on store address *a*. As mentioned before, it is done as part of the *bind* operation.

Let us now think about what constitutes a computation state to be saved in a choice point frame. Upon backtracking, the following information is needed:

- *The argument registers* A1, ..., A*n*, where *n* is the arity of the procedure offering alternative choices of definitions. This is clearly needed as the argument registers, loaded by put instructions with the values of arguments necessary for goal being attempted, are overwritten by executing the chosen clause.

- *The current environment* (value of register E), to recover as a protected environment as explained above.

- *The continuation pointer* (value of register CP), as the current choice will overwrite it.

- *The latest choice point* (value of register B), where to backtrack in case all alternatives offered by the current choice point fail. This acts as the link connecting choice points as a list. It is reinstated as the value of the B register upon discarding the choice point.

- *The next clause*, to try in this definition in case the currently chosen one fails. This slot is updated at each backtracking to this choice point if more alternatives exist.

- *The current trail pointer* (value of register TR), which is needed as the boundary where to *unwind* the trail upon backtracking. If computation comes back to this choice point, this will be the address in the trail down to which all variables that must be reset have been recorded.

- *The current top of heap* (value of register H), which is needed to recover (garbage) heap space of all the structures and variables constructed during the failed attempt which will have resulted in coming back to this choice point.

In summary, a choice point frame is allocated on the stack looking thus:[3]

---

[3]In [War83], David Warren does not include the arity in a choice point, as we do here. He sets up things slightly differently so that this number can always be quickly computed. He can do this by making register B (and the pointers linking the choice point list) reference a choice point frame at its *end*, rather than its *start* as is the case for environment frames. In other words, register B contains the stack address immediately following the latest choice point frame, whereas register E contains the address of the first slot in the environment. Thus, the arity of the latest choice point predicate is always given by $n = B - STACK[B - 4] - 6$. For didactic reasons, we chose to handle E and B identically, judging that saving one stack slot is not really worth the entailed complication of the code implementing the instructions.

| B | $n$ | (*number of arguments*) |
|---|---|---|
| B + 1 | A1 | (*argument register* 1) |

$$\vdots$$

| B + $n$ | An | (*argument register n*) |
|---|---|---|
| B + $n$ + 1 | CE | (*continuation environment*) |
| B + $n$ + 2 | CP | (*continuation pointer*) |
| B + $n$ + 3 | B | (*previous choice point*) |
| B + $n$ + 4 | BP | (*next clause*) |
| B + $n$ + 5 | TR | (*trail pointer*) |
| B + $n$ + 6 | H | (*heap pointer*) |

Note in passing that $\mathcal{M}_2$'s explicit definition for allocate $N$ must be altered in order to work for $\mathcal{M}_3$. This is because the top of stack is now computed differently depending on whether an environment or choice point is the latest frame on the stack. Namely, in $\mathcal{M}_3$:

allocate $N \equiv$ **if** E > B
   **then** *newE* $\leftarrow$ E + STACK[E + 2] + 3
   **else** *newE* $\leftarrow$ B + STACK[B] + 7;
   STACK[*newE*] $\leftarrow$ E;
   STACK[*newE* + 1] $\leftarrow$ CP;
   STACK[*newE* + 2] $\leftarrow$ N;
   E $\leftarrow$ *newE*;
   P $\leftarrow$ P + *instruction_size*(P);

To work with the foregoing choice point format, three new $\mathcal{I}_3$ instructions are added to those already in $\mathcal{I}_{2,}$. They are to deal with the choice point manipulation needed for multiple clause definitions. As expected, these instructions correspond, respectively, to (1) a first, (2) an intermediate (but non ultimate), and (3) a last, clause of a definition. They are:

1. try_me_else $L$
2. retry_me_else $L$
3. trust_me

where $L$ is an instruction label (*i.e.*, an address in the code area). They have for effect, respectively:

1. to allocate a new choice point frame on the stack setting its next clause field to $L$ and the other fields according to the current context, and set B to point to it;

2. having backtracked to the current choice point (indicated by the current value of the B register), to reset all the necessary information from it and update its next clause field to $L$; and,

3. having backtracked to the current choice point, to reset all the necessary information from it, then discard it by resetting B to its predecessor (the value of the link slot).

With this setup, backtracking is effectively handled quite easily. All instructions in which failure may occur (*i.e.*, some unification instructions and all procedure calls) must ultimately test whether failure has indeed occurred. If such is the case, they must then set the instruction counter accordingly. That it, they perform the following operation:

$$backtrack \equiv \text{ P} \leftarrow \text{STACK}[\text{B} + \text{STACK}[\text{B}] + 4];$$

as opposed to having P be unconditionally set to follow its normal (successful) course. Naturally, if no more choice point exists on the stack, this is a terminal failure and execution aborts. All the appropriate alterations of instructions regarding this precaution are given in Appendix B.

The three choice point instructions are defined explicitly in Figures 4.1, 4.2, and 4.3, respectively. In the definition of try_me_else $L$, we use a global variable *num_of_args* giving the arity of the current procedure. This variable is set by call that we must accordingly modify for $\mathcal{M}_3$ from its $\mathcal{M}_2$ form as follows:[4]

$$\text{call } p/n \equiv \text{ CP} \leftarrow \text{P} + instruction\_size(\text{P});$$
$$num\_of\_args \leftarrow n;$$
$$\text{P} \leftarrow @(p/n);$$

As we just explained, we omit treating the case of failure (and therefore of backtracking) where $p/n$ is not defined in this explicit definition of call $p/n$. Its obvious complete form is, as those of all instructions of the full WAM, given in Appendix B.

Finally, the definitions of retry_me_else $L$ and trust_me, use an ancillary operation, *unwind_trail*, to reset all variables since the last choice point to an unbound state. Its explicit definition can be found in Appendix B.

---

[4] As for *num_of_args*, it is legitimate to ask why this is not a global register like E, P, *etc.*, in the design. In fact, the exact manner in which the number of arguments is retrieved at choice point creation time is not at all explained in [War83, War88]. Moreover, upon private inquiry, David H. D. Warren could not remember whether that was an incidental omission. So we chose to introduce this global variable as opposed to a register as no such explicit register was specified for the original WAM.

---

try_me_else $L \equiv$ **if** E $>$ B
               **then** $newB \leftarrow$ E + STACK[E + 2] + 3
               **else** $newB \leftarrow$ B + STACK[B] + 7;
               STACK[$newB$] $\leftarrow$ $num\_of\_args$;
               $n \leftarrow$ STACK[$newB$];
               **for** $i \leftarrow 1$ **to** $n$ **do** STACK[$newB + i$] $\leftarrow$ A$i$;
               STACK[$newB + n + 1$] $\leftarrow$ E;
               STACK[$newB + n + 2$] $\leftarrow$ CP;
               STACK[$newB + n + 3$] $\leftarrow$ B;
               STACK[$newB + n + 4$] $\leftarrow$ $L$;
               STACK[$newB + n + 5$] $\leftarrow$ TR;
               STACK[$newB + n + 6$] $\leftarrow$ H;
               B $\leftarrow$ $newB$;
               HB $\leftarrow$ H;
               P $\leftarrow$ P + $instruction\_size$(P);

---

**Figure 4.1**

$\mathcal{M}_3$ choice point instruction try_me_else

---

retry_me_else $L \equiv$ $n \leftarrow$ STACK[B];
                  **for** $i \leftarrow 1$ **to** $n$ **do** A$i \leftarrow$ STACK[B + $i$];
                  E $\leftarrow$ STACK[B + $n$ + 1];
                  CP $\leftarrow$ STACK[B + $n$ + 2];
                  STACK[B + $n$ + 4] $\leftarrow$ $L$;
                  $unwind\_trail$(STACK[B + $n$ + 5], TR);
                  TR $\leftarrow$ STACK[B + $n$ + 5];
                  H $\leftarrow$ STACK[B + $n$ + 6];
                  HB $\leftarrow$ H;
                  P $\leftarrow$ P + $instruction\_size$(P);

---

**Figure 4.2**

$\mathcal{M}_3$ choice point instruction retry_me_else

---

```
trust_me ≡  n ← STACK[B];
            for i ← 1 to n do Ai ← STACK[B + i];
            E ← STACK[B + n + 1];
            CP ← STACK[B + n + 2];
            unwind_trail(STACK[B + n + 5], TR);
            TR ← STACK[B + n + 5];
            H ← STACK[B + n + 6];
            B ← STACK[B + n + 3];
            HB ← STACK[B + n + 6];
            P ← P + instruction_size(P);
```

---

**Figure 4.3**

$\mathcal{M}_3$ choice point instruction trust_me

In conclusion, there are three patterns of code translations for a procedure definition in $\mathcal{L}_3$, depending on whether it has one, two, or more than two clauses. The code generated in the first case is identical to what is generated for an $\mathcal{L}_2$ program on $\mathcal{M}_2$. In the second case, the pattern for a procedure $p/n$ is:

$p/n$   :   try_me_else $L$
           *code for first clause*
$L$    :   trust_me
           *code for second clause*

and for the last case:

$p/n$   :   try_me_else $L_1$
           *code for first clause*
$L_1$   :   retry_me_else $L_2$
           *code for second clause*
               ⋮
$L_{k-1}$  :   retry_me_else $L_k$
           *code for penultimate clause*
$L_k$   :   trust_me
           *code for last clause*

where each clause is translated as it would be as a single $\mathcal{L}_2$ clause for $\mathcal{M}_2$. For example, $\mathcal{M}_3$ code for the definition:

```
p/2  :  try_me_else L₁            %  p
        get_variable X3, A1       %     (X,
        get_structure a/0, A2     %         a)
        proceed                   %             .

L₁   :  retry_me_else L₂          %  p
        get_structure b/0, A1     %     (b,
        get_variable X3, A2       %         X)
        proceed                   %             .

L₂   :  trust_me                  %
        allocate 1                %  p
        get_variable X3, A1       %     (X,
        get_variable Y1, A2       %         Y) :-
        put_value X3, A1          %                p(X,
        put_structure a/0, A2     %                    a
        call p/2                  %                     ),
        put_structure b/0, A1     %                p(b,
        put_value Y1, A2          %                    Y
        call p/2                  %                     )
        deallocate                %                      .
```

**Figure 4.4**
$\mathcal{M}_3$ code for a multiple clause definition

$p(X, a).$
$p(b, X).$
$p(X, Y) :- p(X, a), p(b, Y).$

is given in Figure 4.4.

**Exercise 4.1** Trace the execution of $\mathcal{L}_3$ query $?-p(c, d)$ with code in Figure 4.4, giving all the successive states of the stack, the heap, and the trail.

**Exercise 4.2** It is possible to maintain separate AND-stack and OR-stack. Discuss the alterations that would be needed to the foregoing setup to do so, ensuring a correct management of environments and choice points.

# 5 Optimizing the Design

Now that the reader is hopefully convinced that the design we have reached forms an adequate target language and architecture for compiling pure Prolog, we can begin transforming it in order to recover Warren's machine as an ultimate design. Therefore, since all optimizations considered here are part of the definitive design, we shall now refer to the abstract machine gradually being elaborated as the WAM. In the process, we shall abide by a few principles of design pervasively motivating all the conception features of the WAM. We will repeatedly invoke these principles in design decisions as we progress toward the full WAM engine, as more evidence justifying them accrues.

> **WAM Principle 1** *Heap space is to be used as sparingly as possible, as terms built on the heap turn out to be relatively persistent.*

> **WAM Principle 2** *Registers must be allocated in such a way as to avoid unnecessary data movement, and minimize code size as well.*

> **WAM Principle 3** *Particular situations that occur very often, even though correctly handled by general-case instructions, are to be accommodated by special ones if space and/or time may be saved thanks to their specificity.*

In the light of WAM Principles 1, 2, and 3, we may now improve on $\mathcal{M}_3$.

## 5.1 Heap representation

As many readers of [AK90] did, this reader may have wondered about the necessity of the extra level of indirection systematically introduced in the heap by an STR cell for *each* functor symbol. In particular, Fernando Pereira [Per90] suggested that instead of that shown in Figure 2.1 on Page 7, a more economical heap representation for $p(Z, h(Z, W), f(W))$ ought to be that of Figure 5.1, where reference to the term from elsewhere must be from a store (or register) cell of the form $\langle$ STR , 5 $\rangle$. In other words, there is actually no need to allot a systematic STR cell before each functor cell.

As it turns out, only one tiny modification of one instruction is needed in order to accommodate this more compact representation. Namely, the put_structure instruction is simplified to:

| 0 | $h/2$ | |
|---|-------|---|
| 1 | REF | 1 |
| 2 | REF | 2 |
| 3 | $f/1$ | |
| 4 | REF | 2 |
| 5 | $p/3$ | |
| 6 | REF | 1 |
| 7 | STR | 0 |
| 8 | STR | 3 |

**Figure 5.1**

Better heap representation for term $p(Z, h(Z, W), f(W))$

$$\text{put\_structure } f/n, \text{X}i \equiv \quad \text{HEAP}[\text{H}] \leftarrow f/n;$$
$$\text{X}i \leftarrow \langle \text{STR}, \text{H} \rangle;$$
$$\text{H} \leftarrow \text{H} + 1;$$

Clearly, this is not only in complete congruence with WAM Principle 1, but it also eliminates unnecessary levels of indirection and hence speeds up dereferencing.

The main reason for our not having used this better heap representation in Section 2.1 was essentially didactic, wishing to avoid having to mention references from outside the heap (*e.g.*, from registers) before due time. In addition, we did not bother bringing up this optimization in [AK90] as we are doing here, as we had not realized that so little was in fact needed to incorporate it.[1]

---

[1] After dire reflection seeded by discussions with Fernando Pereira, we eventually realized that this optimization was indeed cheap—a fact that had escaped our attention. We are grateful to him for pointing this out. However, he himself warns [Per90]:

"Now, this representation (which, I believe, is the one used by Quintus, SICStus Prolog, *etc.*) has indeed some disadvantages:

1. If there aren't enough tags to distinguish functor cells from the other cells, garbage collection becomes trickier, because a pointed-to value does not in general identify its own type (only the pointer does).

2. If you want to use [the Huet-Fages] circular term unification algorithm, redirecting pointers becomes messy, for the [same] reason...

In fact, what [the term representation in Section 2.1 is] doing is enforcing a convention that makes every functor application tagged as such by the appearance of a STR cell just before the functor word."

## 5.2  Constants, lists, and anonymous variables

To be fully consistent with the complete WAM unification instruction set and in accordance with WAM Principle 3, we introduce special instructions for the specific handling of 0-ary structures (*i.e.*, constants), lists, and variables which appear only once within a scope—so-called *anonymous* variables. These enhancements will also be in the spirit of WAM Principles 1 and 2 as savings in heap space, code size, and data movement will ensue.

Constants and lists are, of course, well handled by the structure oriented get, put, and unify instructions. However, work and space are wasted in the process, that need not really be. Consider the case of constants as, for instance, the code in Figure 2.10, on Page 19. There, the sequence of instructions:

```
unify_variable X7
get_structure a/0, X7
```

simply binds a register and proceeds to check the presence of, or build, the constant $a$ on the heap. Clearly, one register can be saved and data movement optimized with one specialized instruction: unify_constant $a$. The same situation in a query would simplify a sequence:

```
put_structure c/0, Xi
set_variable Xi
```

into one specialized instruction set_constant $c$. Similarly, put and get instructions can thus be specialized from those of structures to deal specifically with constants. Thus, we define a new sort of data cells tagged CON, indicating that the cell's datum is a constant. For example, a heap representation starting at address 10 for the structure $f(b, g(a))$ could be:

| 8  | $g/1$ |   |
|----|-------|---|
| 9  | CON   | $a$ |
| 10 | $f/2$ |   |
| 11 | CON   | $b$ |
| 12 | STR   | 8 |

**Exercise 5.1**  Could the following (smaller) heap representation starting at address 10 be an alternative for the structure $f(b, g(a))$? Why?

| 10 | $f/2$ | |
|----|-------|---|
| 11 | CON | $b$ |
| 12 | $g/1$ | |
| 13 | CON | $a$ |

Heap space for constants can also be saved when loading a register with, or binding a variable to, a constant. Rather than systematically occupying a heap cell to reference, a constant can be simply assigned as a literal value. The following instructions are thus added to $\mathcal{I}_0$:

1. put_constant $c, \mathrm{X}i$
2. get_constant $c, \mathrm{X}i$
3. set_constant $c$
4. unify_constant $c$

and are explicitly defined in Figure 5.2.

Programming with linear lists being so privileged in Prolog, it makes sense to tailor the design for this specific structure. In particular, non-empty list functors need not be represented explicitly on the heap. Thus again, we define a fourth sort for heap cells tagged LIS, indicating that the cell's datum is the heap address of the first element of a list pair. Clearly, to respect the subterm contiguity convention, the second of the pair is always at the address following that of the first. The following instructions (defined explicitly in Figure 5.3) are thus added to $\mathcal{I}_0$:

1. put_list $\mathrm{X}i$
2. get_list $\mathrm{X}i$

For example, the code generated for query $?-p(Z, [Z, W], f(W))$., using Prolog's notation for lists, is shown in Figure 5.4    and that for fact $p(f(X), [Y, f(a)], Y)$., in Figure 5.5. Note the hidden presence of the atom [] as list terminator.

Of course, having introduced specially tagged data cells for constants and non-empty lists will require adapting accordingly the general-purpose unification algorithm given in Figure 2.7. The reader will find the complete algorithm in appendix Section B.2, on Page 104.

> **Exercise 5.2** In [War83], Warren also uses special instructions put_nil $\mathrm{X}i$, get_nil $\mathrm{X}i$, and to handle the list terminator constant ([]). Define the effect of these instructions, and give explicit pseudo-code implementing them. Discuss their worth being provided as opposed to using put_constant [], $\mathrm{X}i$, put_constant [], $\mathrm{X}i$, set_constant [], and unify_constant [].

```
put_constant c, Xi ≡  Xi ← ⟨ CON , c ⟩;


get_constant c, Xi ≡  addr ← deref(Xi);
                      case STORE [addr] of
                          ⟨ REF , _ ⟩  :  STORE [addr] ← ⟨ CON , c ⟩;
                                          trail(addr);
                          ⟨ CON , c′ ⟩ :  fail ← (c ≠ c′);
                          other        :  fail ← true;
                      endcase;


set_constant c   ≡  HEAP [H] ← ⟨ CON , c ⟩;
                    H ← H + 1;


unify_constant c ≡  case mode of
                        read  :  addr ← deref(S);
                                 case STORE [addr] of
                                     ⟨ REF , _ ⟩  :  STORE [addr] ← ⟨ CON , c ⟩;
                                                     trail(addr);
                                     ⟨ CON , c′ ⟩ :  fail ← (c ≠ c′);
                                     other        :  fail ← true;
                                 endcase;
                        write :  HEAP [H] ← ⟨ CON , c ⟩;
                                 H ← H + 1;
                    endcase;
```

**Figure 5.2**
Specialized instructions for constants

```
put_list Xi ≡   Xi ← ⟨LIS,H⟩;

get_list Xi ≡   addr ← deref(Xi);
                case STORE[addr] of
                    ⟨REF,_⟩ :  HEAP[H] ← ⟨LIS,H+1⟩;
                               bind(addr, H);
                               H ← H+1;
                               mode ← write;
                    ⟨LIS,a⟩ :  S ← a;
                               mode ← read;
                    other   :  fail ← true;
                endcase;
```

**Figure 5.3**
Specialized instructions for lists

```
put_list X5              %   ?-X5 = [
set_variable X6          %           W|
set_constant []          %              []],
put_variable X4,A1       %      p(Z,
put_list A2              %          [
set_value X4             %           Z|
set_value X5             %             X5],
put_structure f/1,A3     %                 f
set_value X6             %                 (W)
call p/3                 %                    ).
```

**Figure 5.4**
Specialized code for query ?-$p(Z, [Z, W], f(W))$.

```
p/3  :  get_structure f/1, A1   %  p(f
        unify_variable X4        %     (X,
        get_list A2              %        [
        unify_variable X5        %           Y|
        unify_variable X6        %               X6],
        get_value X5, A3         %                   Y),
        get_list X6              %  X6 = [
        unify_variable X7        %         X7|
        unify_constant []        %            []],
        get_structure f/1, X7    %  X7 = f
        unify_constant a         %        (a)
        proceed                  %            .
```

**Figure 5.5**
Specialized code for fact $p(f(X), [Y, f(a)], Y)$.

Last in the rubric of specialized instructions is the case of single-occurrence variables in non-argument positions (*e.g.*, $X$ in Figure 2.4 on Page 11, Figure 2.10 on Page 19, and Figure 5.5 on Page 43). This is worth giving specialized treatment insofar as no register need be allocated for these. In addition, if many occur in a row as in $f(\_, \_, \_)$, say, they can be all be processed in one swoop, saving in generated code size and time. We introduce two new instructions:

1. set_void $n$
2. unify_void $n$

whose effect is, respectively:

1. to push $n$ new unbound REF cells on the heap;
2. in write mode, to behave as set_void $n$ and, in read mode, to skip the next $n$ heap cells starting at location S.

These are given explicitly in Figure 5.6.

Note finally, that an anonymous variable occurring as an argument of the head of a clause can be simply ignored. Then indeed, the corresponding instruction:

get_variable X$i$, A$i$

---

```
set_void n   ≡   for i ← H to H + n − 1 do
                     HEAP [i] ← ⟨REF, i⟩;
                 H ← H + n;

unify_void n ≡   case mode of
                     read  :  S ← S + n;
                     write :  for i ← H to H + n − 1 do
                                  HEAP [i] ← ⟨REF, i⟩;
                              H ← H + n;
                 endcase
```

---

**Figure 5.6**
Anonymous variable instructions

---

```
p/3  :   get_structure g/1, A2    %   p(_, g
         unify_void 1              %        (X),
         get_structure f/3, A3     %              f
         unify_void 3              %                (_, Y, _)
         proceed                   %                        ).
```

---

**Figure 5.7**
Instructions for fact $p(\_, g(X), f(\_, Y, \_))$.

is clearly vacuous. Thus, such instructions are simply eliminated. The code for fact $p(\_, g(X), f(\_, Y, \_))$., for example, shown in Figure 5.7, illustrates this point.

> **Exercise 5.3** What is the machine code generated for the fact $p(\_, \_, \_)$.? What about the *query* $? \text{-} p(\_, \_, \_)$.?

## 5.3  A note on set instructions

Defining the simplistic language $\mathcal{L}_0$ has allowed us to introduce, independently of other Prolog considerations, all WAM instructions dealing with unification. Strictly speaking, the set instructions we have defined are not part of the WAM as described in [War83] or in [War88]. There, one will find that the corresponding `unify` instructions are systematically used where we use `set` instructions. The reason is, as the reader may have noticed, that indeed this is possible provided that the `put_structure` and `put_list` instructions set *mode* to `write`. Then, clearly, all `set` instructions are equivalent to `unify` instructions in `write` mode. We chose to keep these separate as using `set` instructions after `put` instructions is more efficient (it saves mode setting and testing) and makes the code more perspicuous. Moreover, these instructions are more natural, easier to explain and motivate as the data building phase of unification before matching work comes into play.

Incidentally, these instructions together with their `unify` homologues, make "on-the-fly" copying part of unification, resulting in improved space and time consumption, as opposed to the more *naïve* systematic copying of rules before using them.

## 5.4   Register allocation

As in conventional compiler technology, the code generated from the source may give rise to obviously unnecessary data movements. Such can be simplified away by so-called "peep-hole" optimization. This applies to this design as well. Consider for example the *naïve* translation of the fact '$conc([], L, L)$.':

```
conc/3 :   get_constant [], A1   %   conc([],
           get_variable X4, A2   %         L,
           get_value X4, A3      %              L)
           proceed               %                 .
```

Now, there is clearly no need to allocate register X4 for variable $L$ since its only use is to serve as temporary repository—but so can A2. Thus, the `get_variable` becomes `get_variable A2, A2`, and can be eliminated altogether, yielding better code:

```
conc/3 :   get_constant [], A1   %   conc([],
           get_value A2, A3      %         L, L)
           proceed               %                 .
```

More generally, since argument and temporary variable registers are the same, the following instructions are vacuous operations:

```
get_variable Xi, Ai
put_value Xi, Ai
```

```
p/2  :   allocate 2              %   p
         get_variable Y1,A2      %      (X,Y) :-
         put_variable Y2,A2      %                 q(X,Z
         call q/2                %                      ),
         put_value Y2,A1         %                 r(Z,
         put_value Y1,A2         %                    Y
         call r/2                %                      )
         deallocate              %                       .
```

**Figure 5.8**
Better register use for $p(X,Y)$ :- $q(X,Z), r(Z,Y)$.

and can be eliminated. For example, looking back at the example shown in Figure 3.1 on Page 26, we realize that the temporary variable $X$ is the first argument in the head as well as the first atom in the body. Therefore, allocating register X3 to the variable $X$ is clearly silly as it has for consequence the useless movement of the contents of register A1 to X3, then back, as well as two more instructions increasing the code size. Thus, with this observation, it makes sense to allocate register A1 to $X$ and apply the above vacuous operation elimination, resulting in the obviously better instruction sequence shown in Figure 5.8.

Register allocation must try to take advantage of this fact by recognizing situations when appropriate argument registers may also safely be used as temporary variables. Algorithms that do this well can be quite involved. A general method due to Debray [Deb86] works well in reasonable time. A more sophisticated but more (compile-time) expensive technique using Debray's method combined with a reordering of unification instructions can be found in [JDM88]. Register allocation is really auxiliary to the WAM design and can be performed by an independent module in the compiler.

In the sequel, we shall implicitly use this optimization whenever better than *naïve* register allocation can be obviously inferred by the reader.

## 5.5  Last call optimization

The refinement that we introduce next is a generalization of tail-recursion optimization, the effect of which is to turn some recursive procedures into equivalent iterative forms. It is called here *last call optimization* (LCO), as it is applied systematically with or without recursion. If the last procedure call happens to be recursive, then it does amount to tail recursion optimization. However, it is more general as a stack frame recovery process.

The essence of LCO resides in the fact that permanent variables allocated to a rule should no longer be needed by the time all the put instructions preceding the last call in the body are passed. Hence, it is safe to discard the current environment *before* calling the last procedure of the rule's body. This could be achieved quite simply by swapping the call, deallocate sequence that always conclude a rule's instruction sequence (*i.e.*, into deallocate, call).

A consequence of this is that deallocate is never the last instruction in a rule's instruction sequence as it used to be for $\mathcal{M}_2$ and $\mathcal{M}_3$. Therefore, it must be modified accordingly. Namely, it must reset CP, rather than P, to the value of the continuation slot of the current environment being discarded, and set P to continue in sequence. Thus,

$$\texttt{deallocate} \equiv \text{CP} \leftarrow \text{STACK}[\text{E}+1];$$
$$\text{E} \leftarrow \text{STACK}[\text{E}];$$
$$\text{P} \leftarrow \text{P} + \textit{instruction\_size}(\text{P})$$

But then, call being now the last instruction, there is no need for it to set CP. As a matter of fact, it would be wrong if it did since the right continuation will now have been set *a priori* by deallocate. A simple setting of P to the callee's address is all that is needed. We shall not modify call, since it works correctly for non-ultimate procedure calls. Rather, we introduce execute $p/n$, defined as:

$$\texttt{execute } p/n \equiv \textit{num\_of\_args} \leftarrow n;$$
$$\text{P} \leftarrow @(p/n);$$

to be used systematically for the last call in a rule instead of call . To see an example, consider the rule '$p(X,Y) :\texttt{-} q(X,Z), r(Z,Y).$' whose "last call optimized" code is shown in Figure 5.9.

The effect of LCO is subtler than it first appears due to the interleaving of environment and choice point frames on the same stack. Thus, if the topmost frame on the stack is the current environment and not the current choice point (*i.e.*, if $\text{E} > \text{B}$), its space can then be re-used in the next stack allocation (*e.g.*, allocate or try_me_else). This slows downs growth of the stack considerably. On the other hand, if the top of the stack is a choice point, LCO

| $p/2$ | : | `allocate 2`              | % | $p$ |
|-------|---|--------------------------|---|-----|
|       |   | `get_variable Y1,A2`     | % | $(X,Y)$ :- |
|       |   | `put_variable Y2,A2`     | % | $q(X,Z$ |
|       |   | `call q/2`               | % | ), |
|       |   | `put_value Y2,A1`        | % | $r(Z,$ |
|       |   | `put_value Y1,A2`        | % | $Y$ |
|       |   | `deallocate`             | % | ) |
|       |   | `execute r/2`            | % | . |

**Figure 5.9**
$\mathcal{M}_2$ code for $p(X,Y)$ :- $q(X,Z), r(Z,Y)$., with LCO

does not have immediate effect on the stack due to environment protection. In the case where the last call of the last rule is a recursive call, the stack does not grow at all, re-using over and over the exact same space for successive activation frames of the same procedure, resulting in an iterative loop.[2]

## 5.6   Chain rules

A consequence of LCO is that the generated code translating chain rules can be greatly simplified. Indeed, the generic translation of a chain rule of the form '$p(\ldots)$ :- $q(\ldots)$.':

| $p$ | : | `allocate N` |
|-----|---|--------------|
|     |   | *get arguments of p* |
|     |   | *put arguments of q* |
|     |   | `call q` |
|     |   | `deallocate` |

is transformed by LCO into:

---

[2]In pure $\mathcal{L}_2$, this would of course be of little interest since any recursive program would always either fail or loop indefinitely anyway—albeit with a small stack! At any rate, LCO is nonetheless an interesting optimization of execution of (non-recursive) $\mathcal{L}_2$ programs as it keeps stack space well utilized.

```
p :   allocate N
      get arguments of p
      put arguments of q
      deallocate
      execute q
```

Now, note that all variables in a chain rule are necessarily temporary. Hence, the only information which is saved on the stack by an initial `allocate` is the continuation register CP. But this effect of `allocate` is undone before `execute` by `deallocate`. Therefore, this is totally wasted work, and both `allocate` and `deallocate` can be eliminated. Thus, LCO allows translation of the chain rule '$p(\ldots)$ : $-$ $q(\ldots)$.' simply into:

```
p :   get arguments of p
      put arguments of q
      execute q
```

That is, chain rules need no run-time activation frame on the stack at all!

## 5.7   Environment trimming

The correctness of LCO hinges on having observed that permanent variables in the current environment are needed only as long as all the `put` instructions for the last call's arguments are not yet done. This observation can be sharpened by noticing that a permanent variable is in fact no longer needed after the arguments of its ultimate occurrence's goal have all been loaded by `put` instructions. This entails a natural generalization of LCO to allow maximal reuse of stack space at each (*i.e.*, not only the last) call in the body of the rule. More specifically, each permanent variable in the environment can be associated with the goal in which it is used last, and therefore can safely be disposed of before performing the call. The intended effect of such a process is to make the current environment frame's size on the stack shrink gradually, until it eventually vanishes altogether by LCO, this latter optimization being simply the special case of the last goal.

This gradual environment trimming can be made to work automatically by carefully ordering the variables in their environment so as to reflect the ordering of their associated last occurrence goals. Namely, the later a permanent variable's last occurrence's goal is in the body, the lower its offset in the current environment frame is. Thus, the `call` instruction is given a second argument

counting the number of variables still needed in the environment after the
point of call. This count allows later stack allocating instructions to compute
a lower top of stack, if possible. Namely, if the topmost frame on the stack is
the current environment (*i.e.*, if E > B).

Note that the explicit definition of allocate again needs to be changed
from what it was for $\mathcal{M}_3$. In order to reflect a correct value at all times, the
offset that it gets from the preceding environment must be updated by each
trimming call. In fact, such updates are not needed. Since a more precise
environment stack offset is now explicitly passed as an argument to call's,
the argument of allocate becomes superfluous. Indeed, the offset can be
dynamically retrieved by allocate (and try_me_else) as a consequence
of the following fact: *the continuation slot of the latest environment frame,*
STACK[E + 1], *always contains the address of the instruction immediately*
*following the appropriate* call P, N *instruction where N is precisely the*
*desired offset.* Hence, allocate no longer takes an argument, and an
environment frame no longer needs an offset slot. Instead, the right offset is
calculated by allocate as CODE[STACK[E + 1] − 1].[3]

With this simplification, an environment frame on top of the stack now looks
thus:

| E | CE | (*continuation environment*) |
|---|---|---|
| E + 1 | CP | (*continuation point*) |
| E + 2 | Y1 | (*permanent variable* 1) |
| | | ⋮ |

and the (now definitive) definition of allocate is:[4]

allocate ≡ **if** E > B
          **then** *newE* ← E + CODE[STACK[E + 1] − 1] + 2
          **else** *newE* ← B + STACK[B] + 7;
          STACK[*newE*] ← E;
          STACK[*newE* + 1] ← CP;
          E ← *newE*;
          P ← P + *instruction_size*(P);

---

[3]Recall that by CODE[*i*], we mean the contents of STORE[*i*] in the code area at address *i*.
This works under the (reasonable) assumption that an integer occupies one memory word.

[4]Note incidentally, that a similar alteration must be done for try_me_else. The definitive
version for that instruction is given in Appendix B.

The rule '$p(X,Y,Z)$ :- $q(U,V,W), r(Y,Z,U), s(U,W), t(X,V)$.', for example, is one in which all variables are permanent. The last occurrence's goal of each variable is given in the following table, along with a consistent ordering assigning to each a $Yi$ indexed by its offset in the environment frame:

| Variable | Last goal | Offset |
|----------|-----------|--------|
| $X$ | $t$ | Y1 |
| $Y$ | $r$ | Y5 |
| $Z$ | $r$ | Y6 |
| $U$ | $s$ | Y3 |
| $V$ | $t$ | Y2 |
| $W$ | $s$ | Y4 |

That is, after the CE and CP slots, $X, V, U, W, Y, Z$ come in this order in the environment. Environment trimming code for this rule is shown in Figure 5.10.

## 5.8   Stack variables

Recall that, according to WAM Principle 1, allocation of heap space is to be avoided whenever possible. Thus, we may go even farther in optimizing austerity in the case of a permanent variable which first occurs in the body of a rule as a goal argument. From what we have seen, such a variable $Yn$ is initialized with a put_variable $Yn, Ai$ which sets both the environment slot $Yn$ and argument register $Ai$ to point to a newly allocated unbound REF heap cell (see Figure 2.8, on Page 18). Now, since $Yn$ is to be treated as a local variable, it has been allocated a cell in the environment which is to exist during this rule's body execution—assuming, for the time being, that environment trimming or LCO are not performed. So why not save, rather than systematically waste, that (global) heap cell? More specifically, a more appropriate semantics for the put_variable instruction, when used on a permanent variable, ought to be:

$$\text{put\_variable } Yn, Ai \equiv \quad addr \leftarrow \text{E} + n + 1;$$
$$\text{STACK}[addr] \leftarrow \langle \text{REF}, addr \rangle;$$
$$Ai \leftarrow \text{STACK}[addr];$$

That is, it should not allocate a heap cell as done for a temporary register.

Unfortunately, there are rather insidious consequences to this apparently innocuous change as it interferes with environment trimming and LCO. The

```
p/3  :  allocate             %  p
        get_variable Y1, A1  %    (X,
        get_variable Y5, A2  %      Y,
        get_variable Y6, A3  %         Z) :-
        put_variable Y3, A1  %                   q(U,
        put_variable Y2, A2  %                     V,
        put_variable Y4, A3  %                       W
        call q/3, 6          %                         ),
        put_value Y5, A1     %                   r(Y,
        put_value Y6, A2     %                     Z,
        put_value Y3, A3     %                       U
        call r/3, 4          %                         ),
        put_value Y3, A1     %                   s(U,
        put_value Y4, A2     %                     W
        call s/2, 2          %                         ),
        put_value Y1, A1     %                   t(X,
        put_value Y2, A2     %                     V
        deallocate           %                       )
        execute t/2          %                          .
```

**Figure 5.10**

Environment trimming code

trouble then is that environment variables may be disposed of while still unbound. Therefore, any reference to an unbound stack variable runs the risk of potential catastrophe, becoming a dangling reference upon careless discarding of the variable. As a result, it is no longer correct to let the *bind* operation set an arbitrary direction when establishing a reference between two unbound variables. More pathologically, the following instructions have now become incorrect if used blindly in some situations: `put_value` and `set_value` (thus also `unify_value` in `write` mode).

The following three subsections treat each problem by (1) first giving a correct binding convention, then (2) analyzing what may go wrong with `put_value`, and (3) with `set_value` and `unify_value`, explaining how to repair the trouble.

### 5.8.1  Variable binding and memory layout

Three cases of variable-variable bindings are possible: (1) heap-heap, (2) stack-stack, and (3) heap-stack. In Case (1), as alluded to before on Page 14, when the *bind* operation is performed on two unbound (heap) addresses, which of the two is made to reference the other does not affect correctness. However, making an arbitrary choice does affect performance as it may lead to much more work than necessary by causing more variable trailing and resetting than may be needed. Consider for example two heap variables, one before HB and the other after HB. Making the first reference the second requires trailing it (and its potential subsequent resetting) while the contrary is unconditional and requires none.

In Cases (2) and (3), the symptoms are quite more serious as which direction the binding occurs can be incorrect due to potential discarding of stack variables. For example, the rule '$p(X,X)$ :- $q(X), r(X)$.' invoked with '?-$p(Y,Z)$.' will not work correctly if $Y$ is bound to $X$ since $q/1$ may leave the stack variable $X$ unbound. The other direction is the only correct one. As it turns out, most correct bindings can be ensured following a simple chronological reference rule:

> **WAM Binding Rule 1** *Always make the variable of higher address reference that of lower address.*

In other words, an older (less recently created) variable cannot reference a younger (more recently created) variable.

Let us examine what is gained. In Case (1), as explained above, unconditional bindings are thus favored over conditional ones, avoiding unnecessary trailing and resulting in swift heap space recovery upon backtracking.

In Case (2), WAM Binding Rule 1 rule is also clearly beneficial for the same reasons as for Case (1). It happens to be also consistent with the ordering among variables within a single environment set up to allow environment trimming. This is all the better. Unfortunately, this rule is not sufficient to prevent dangling references in a stack-stack binding as will be seen in the next subsection.

In Case (3), the problem (as exposed in the next two subsections) is that stack space is volatile while heap space is persistent, making references to the stack potentially dangerous. Clearly, it would be a source of complication ever to establish a binding from the heap toward the stack, whereas the contrary presents no problem. Therefore, the WAM enforces the following:

> **WAM Binding Rule 2** *Heap variables must <u>never</u> be set to a reference into the stack.*

To suit this, the WAM organizes its memory layout specifically so that WAM Binding Rule 1 is naturally consistent with:

> **WAM Binding Rule 3** *The stack must be allocated at higher addresses than the heap, in the same global address space.*

This must be done, of course, allowing sufficient slack for growth of the heap. This rule entails forbidding the participation of stack variables in a reference chain in any way other than grouped as a subchain prefix. That is, a reference chain containing any stack variables at all will have them all appear contiguously and early in the chain. Then, discarding a stack variable cannot break a chain. (This is guaranteed in the subchain prefix of stack variables by WAM Binding Rule 1.)

However, we see next that this rule is violated by some instructions (put_value, set_value, and unify_value). We presently examine this and adapt the design so that no incorrect binding may ever occur.

### 5.8.2  Unsafe variables

A stack variable is discarded before calling the goal in which it last occurs although it may still be unbound or bound to another unbound permanent variable in the same (current) environment (*i.e.*, one which is to be also disposed of). Clearly, the danger is then that the call may refer to the discarded variables. For this reason, a permanent variable which is initialized by a

```
⟨0⟩  p/1  :   allocate              %   p
⟨1⟩            get_variable Y1,A1   %     (X):-
⟨2⟩            put_variable Y2,A1   %          q(Y,
⟨3⟩            put_value Y1,A2      %             X
⟨4⟩            call q/2,2           %               ),
⟨5⟩            put_value Y2,A1      %          r(Y,
⟨6⟩            put_value Y1,A2      %             X
⟨7⟩            deallocate           %               )
⟨8⟩            execute r/2          %                 .
```

**Figure 5.11**
Unsafe code for $p(X) :- q(Y, X), r(Y, X)$.

put_variable (*i.e.*, which first occurs as the argument of a body goal) is called an *unsafe* variable.

Let us take an example with the rule '$p(X) :- q(Y, X), r(Y, X)$.' in which both $X$ and $Y$ are permanent variables, but only $Y$ is unsafe. This is because $Y$ is initialized with a put_variable (since its first occurrence is in a body goal) while $X$, first occurring in the head, is initialized with a get_variable. Figure 5.11 shows the (incorrect) translation as it is done in our current setting. Let us trace what happens when put_value Y2,A1 is used on Line 5. Let us assume that $p$ is called with an unbound variable; that is, with the sequence of the form:

```
put_variable Xi,A1
execute p/1
```

Thus, at the point right before Line 0, A1 points to the heap address (say, 36) of an unbound REF cell at the top of the heap. Then, allocate creates an environment on the stack (where, say, Y1 is at address 77 and Y2 at address 78 in the stack). Line 1 sets STACK[77] to ⟨REF, 36⟩, and Line 2 sets A1 (and STACK[78]) to ⟨REF, 78⟩. Line 3 sets A2 to the value of STACK[77]; that is, ⟨REF, 36⟩. Let us assume that the call to $q$ on Line 4 does not affect these settings at all (*e.g.*, the fact $q(\_,\_)$ is defined). Then, (the wrong) Line 5 would set A1 to ⟨REF, 78⟩, and Line 6 sets A2 to ⟨REF, 36⟩. Next, deallocate throws away STACK[77] and STACK[78]. Suppose now that the code for $r$ starts with an allocate re-using stack space 77 and 78 then, lo!, the get instructions of $r$ will find nonsensical data in A1.

Note however that an unsafe variable's binding can easily be checked at run-time so that trouble may be averted on the fly by taking appropriate measures only if needed. Let us reflect on the possible situations of a given unsafe variable $Yn$ in the last goal where it occurs. There are two cases that will need attention: (1) when $Yn$ appears only as an argument of its last goal; and, (2) when $Yn$ appears in that goal nested in a structure, whether or not it is also an argument. We will treat later the second case, as it interacts with a more general source of unsafety that we shall analyze after treating the first case.

So let us consider for now the case where all occurrences of unsafe $Yn$ are arguments of the last goal where $Yn$ appears. That is, all these correspond to put_value $Yn, Ai$ instructions. As explained, it is desirable to ensure that a run-time check be carried out verifying that no reference chain leading to $Yn$ eventually points to an unbound slot in the environment. The solution is to use a modification of the effect of put_value $Yn, Ai$ to ascertain this. More specifically, let us call this modified instruction put_unsafe_value $Yn, Ai$. It behaves exactly like put_value $Yn, Ai$ if the reference chain from $Yn$ does not lead to an unbound variable in the current environment. If it does, then this altered instruction binds the referenced stack variable to a new unbound REF cell pushed on the heap, and sets $Ai$ to point to that cell. Explicitly,[5]

$$\text{put\_unsafe\_value } Yn, Ai \equiv \quad addr \leftarrow deref(\text{E} + n + 1);$$

$$\textbf{if } addr < \text{E}$$
$$\textbf{then } Ai \leftarrow \text{STORE}[addr]$$
$$\textbf{else}$$
$$\quad \textbf{begin}$$
$$\quad\quad \text{HEAP}[\text{H}] \leftarrow \langle \text{REF}, \text{H} \rangle;$$
$$\quad\quad bind(addr, \text{H});$$
$$\quad\quad Ai \leftarrow \text{HEAP}[\text{H}];$$
$$\quad\quad \text{H} \leftarrow \text{H} + 1$$
$$\quad \textbf{end};$$

Looking back at the example of Figure 5.11, if Line 5 is not as shown but replaced with put_unsafe_value $Y2, A1$, then HEAP [37] is created and

---

[5]Note incidentally that having a global address space with the relative memory layout of the stack being allocated at higher addresses than the heap has as a nice consequence to make it quite easy to test whether $Yn$'s value is an unbound variable in the current environment with a mere comparison of memory addresses. Strictly speaking, this test is not quite correct because *deref* may actually yield the address of an X register containing a literal constant. To prevent this trivial point from complicating matters unnecessarily, we may assume that X registers conveniently reside at the highest end of the global store.

set to $\langle$ REF , 37 $\rangle$, STACK[78] and A1 are set to $\langle$ REF , 37 $\rangle$, then A2 is set
to $\langle$ REF , 36 $\rangle$ (the value of STACK[77]) on the following line. Discarding
STACK[77] and STACK[78] is now quite safe as executing $r$ will get correct
values from A1 and A2.

The question still remaining is to decide which among several occurrences
of put_value Y$n$, A$i$ must be replaced with the safety check modification for
a given unsafe Y$n$. In fact, it is sufficient to replace only *one* of them, although
not an arbitrary one but, quite importantly, the *first occurrence in this last goal*.
To see this on an example, consider the clause:[6]

$p$ :- $q(X), r(X, X)$.

If the safety check is done last, as in:

```
p/0 :  allocate
       put_variable Y1,A1
       call q/1,1
       put_value Y1,A1
       put_unsafe_value Y1,A2
       deallocate
       execute r/2
```

then argument register will still contain a reference to the discarded environment
when $r/2$ is called. Therefore, the following is the only possible correct code:

```
p/0 :  allocate
       put_variable Y1,A1
       call q/1,1
       put_unsafe_value Y1,A1
       put_value Y1,A2
       deallocate
       execute r/2
```

It has the effect of "globalizing" the value of Y1 so as to guarantee that it may
be discarded without leaving a nonsensical reference in A1.

---

[6]This example is due to Michael Hanus [Han90] and, independently, to Pascal van Hentenryck [vH90]. Both pointed out to this author the incorrect replacement rule described (as that of
the *last* occurrence of an unsafe variable) in [AK90]. In fact, the incorrect rule in [AK90] had
been simply inherited verbatim from Warren's original report [War83] (Page 14, Line 3), and later
explained by him as follows [War90]:

"I agree that this is ambiguous or misleading. I think it may be partly explained by the fact that
the memo (tacitly?) assumes that goal arguments are compiled in reverse order and therefore the
last arguments will be compiled first!"

### 5.8.3 Nested stack references

When an unsafe variable occurs in its last goal nested in a structure (*i.e.*, with a corresponding set_value or a unify_value), the situation pertains to a more general pathology which may affect temporary variables as well. Consider the rule '$a(X)$ :- $b(f(X))$.' for example. As we have it, this is translated thus:

$a/1$ :   get_variable X2, A1
          put_structure $f/1$, A1
          set_value X2
          execute $b/1$

Let us consider now the query '? - $a(X), c(X)$.' being translated as:

          allocate
          put_variable Y1, A1
          call $a/1, 1$

                $\vdots$

and let us examine in detail what happens during execution. Before the call to $a/1$, a stack frame containing the variable Y1 is allocated and initialized to unbound by put_variable Y1, A1. The code of $a/1$ begins by setting X2 to reference that stack slot (the value of A1), and pushes the functor $f/1$ on the heap. Then, behold!, set_value X2 pushes the value of X2 onto the heap, establishing a reference from the heap to the stack. This violates WAM Binding Rule 2 and creates a source of disaster when Y1 is eventually discarded.

Of course, the same ill-fated behavior plagues unify_value as its write mode semantics is identical to set_value's. Then, the question is: When can it be statically guaranteed that set_value (resp., unify_value) will not create an unwanted heap-to-stack reference? The answer is: Any time its argument has not been explicitly initialized to be on the heap in the given clause. Then indeed, the first set_value (resp., unify_value) performed on it may cause potential havoc. Specifically, set_value V$n$ (resp., unify_value V$n$) is unsafe whenever the variable V$n$ has *not* been initialized in this clause with set_variable or unify_variable, nor, if V$n$ is temporary, with put_variable.

Again, the cure amounts to performing appropriate run-time checks which can trigger dynamic globalizing of a guilty stack variable whenever needed.

Namely, the *first* set_value (resp., unify_value) instruction of the clause to be performed on a variable which is not guaranteed to lead to the heap (*i.e.*, meeting the explicit conditions described in the previous paragraph), must be replaced with a new one, set_local_value (resp., unify_local_value, behaving like unify_value in read mode), which tests whether the dereferenced value resides in the heap or in the stack. If the dereferenced value is an unbound heap address, it behaves as set_value (resp., as unify_value in write mode); *i.e.*, it pushes it on the heap. If the dereferenced value is an unbound stack address, it pushes a new unbound heap cell and binds the stack variable to it. Explicitly,[7]

$$\texttt{set\_local\_value } Vn \equiv \ \ addr \leftarrow deref(Vn);$$
$$\textbf{if } addr < \texttt{H}$$
$$\textbf{then } \texttt{HEAP[H]} \leftarrow \texttt{HEAP}[addr]$$
$$\textbf{else}$$
$$\textbf{begin}$$
$$\texttt{HEAP[H]} \leftarrow \langle \texttt{REF}, \texttt{H} \rangle;$$
$$bind(addr, \texttt{H})$$
$$\textbf{end};$$
$$\texttt{H} \leftarrow \texttt{H} + 1;$$

An explicit expression for unify_local_value is readily derived from the definition of unify_value (given in Figure 2.6, on Page 13) by replacing the body of the write mode case with the above code.

If set_local_value X2 replaces set_value X2 in the example above, it will realize that the value of X2 is a stack address and then bind it to a new unbound cell on the heap. This maintains a stack-to-heap reference, and WAM Binding Rule 2 is respected.

As a final observation, let us consider the particular case where an unsafe variable Yn occurs both as an argument of its last goal and also nested in a structure somewhere in the same clause. Then, it is only necessary to make the appropriate change to whichever instruction comes first between the last goal's put_value Yn, Ai's and the clause's set_value Yn's (resp., unify_value Yn's). This is because changing the first such instruction will ensure that the variable is safely globalized for the other, making the run-time check unnecessary at that later point.

---

[7]See Footnote 5 at the bottom of Page 56.

## 5.9   Variable classification revisited

At this point, the time is ripe for setting things right about the definition
of temporary and permanent variables. In our opinion, the way the WAM
classifies variables is perhaps the most puzzling item to justify for the learning
reader. Indeed, although the definition we have used thus far is correct as
given, it is not exactly that given and used in [War83] or [War88]. We presently
analyze this discrepancy and discuss in particular the motivation, as well as
some rather subtle consequences, of the original WAM designer's definition.

In fact, our definition and justification of variable classification take David
H. D. Warren's actual conception back to front. In his view, a permanent
variable is simply a conventional local variable. Therefore, *all* variables
appearing in a clause are *a priori* permanent variables; *i.e.*, local variables to
be allocated on the stack. This is because a local variable's lifetime ought
to be that of the activation of the clause in which it occurs. On the other
hand, allocating a variable on the heap would entail making it a global variable
insofar as computation does not backtrack to a previous choice point. However,
some variables in a clause need not be allocated on the stack, either because
they are initialized with previously existing data or because they must be part
of a structure on the heap. Obviously, these considerations call for a careful
reformulation of variable classification.

Warren's original definition is as follows:

> **Warren's variable classification**  A temporary variable *is one*
> *which does not occur in more than one body goal (counting the*
> *head as part of the first body goal)* and *first occurs in the head,*
> *or in a structure, or in the last goal.* A permanent variable *is one*
> *which is not temporary.*

First of all, let us observe that both our and Warren's classification consider
permanent any variable occurring in more than one body goal. However,
whereas this criterion is a necessary and sufficient characterization of permanent
variables by our definition, it is only a sufficient one for Warren's. Now, from
our presentation, let us try to recover and justify Warren's variable classification.

The point is to restrict our definition of temporary variables (and thus broaden
that of permanent variables) to minimize heap allocation, and consequently the
size of global data. As we saw, local variables are quite thriftily managed by
environment trimming and LCO, and therefore offer a preferable alternative
to X registers whenever possible. Therefore, in order to abide by Warren's

view, we must completely change our perspective and consider that *a variable is permanent by default unless it is required to be explicitly allocated on the heap*.

The question now, is: When does a non-void variable originally deemed temporary in our definition (*i.e.*, occurring in no more than one body goal) *really* require to be systematically allocated in the heap? Memory allocation for a variable happens, if at all, at its first occurrence in the clause. Let us now analyze all possible situations of first occurrence.

If the first occurrence is in the head of the rule, then the variable is either an argument, and therefore bound to an already existing cell on the heap, or deeper in the stack; or, it is nested in a structure and hence will necessarily be allocated on the heap by the unification instructions. This is the case because the convention is that a functor cell on the heap must be followed by as many cells as its arity dictates. As a result, a head variable never requires stack space allocation. Therefore, it is sufficient to manipulate it through an X register; *i.e.*, treat it as a temporary variable.

For the same reasons, if the first occurrence is nested inside a structure in the body, then a heap cell will necessarily be allocated for it by the unification instructions. So it might as well be treated as a temporary variable, saving a stack slot.

Another clear case is when the first occurrence of the variable is as an argument in the *last* body goal. Then indeed, since performing LCO will require systematically globalizing it anyway, it makes more sense to treat it as a temporary variable.

The foregoing situations cover all those in Warren's definition of a *temporary* variable. Therefore, the criteria for that part of the definition which characterizes a temporary variable are justifiably sound. But is this true for Warren's definition of a *permanent* variable? Indeed, there is one last situation not covered by our foregoing analysis; namely, the case of a variable occurring only in one body goal which is neither the first nor the last goal. As it turns out, unfortunately, *Warren's variable classification is inconsistent with environment trimming, even with the setup of run-time checks that we have explained in the previous sections.*

Let us argue with a specific example.[8] Consider the rule '$a : - b(X, X), c.$'. According to our definition, $X$ is treated as a temporary variable. This results

---

[8]The lame behavior of this example was pointed out to the author by Damian Chu [Chu90] and Michael Hanus [Han90].

```
a/0  :   allocate              %   a :-
         put_variable A1,A2     %        b(X, X
         call b/2,0             %                 ),
         deallocate            %        c
         execute c/0           %           .
```

**Figure 5.12**
Code for $a$ :- $b(X, X), c.$, by our classification

```
a/0  :   allocate                    %   a :-
         put_variable Y1,A1          %        b(X,
         put_unsafe_value Y1,A2      %            X
         call b/2,0                  %                  ),
         deallocate                 %        c
         execute c/0                %           .
```

**Figure 5.13**
Code for $a$ :- $b(X, X), c.$, by Warren's classification

in the compiled code shown as Figure 5.12, where $X$ is correctly handled as a temporary variable, admittedly at the expense of systematically allocating a heap slot for it.

On the other hand, according to Warren's variable classification, the variable $X$ is a *permanent variable*. Therefore, following the compilation rules described in the previous sections, the generated code would be that shown in Figure 5.13. Now, observe what happens when calling $a$ with the instruction sequence of Figure 5.13. A stack slot is allocated for Y1, then register A1 is made to point to that slot. Then, a run-time check is carried out because Y1 is unsafe and it is found that Y1 must be globalized. This is done, making both Y1 and A2 point to a new heap cell. Then, $b/2$ is called after trimming Y1 out of the environment. However, *register A1 still points to the discarded slot!* It is therefore clear that for Warren's classification to be correct, something must be done to prevent this particular ailment.

As far as this author could read, it has not been explained anywhere (including in [War83, War88]) how to prevent incorrect code as that of Figure 5.13 to be generated because of Warren's classification, let alone what correct code

```
a/0  :  allocate              %  a :-
         put_variable Y1,A1    %      b(X,
         put_value Y1,A2       %         X
         call b/2,1            %            ),
         deallocate            %      c
         execute c/0           %       .
```

**Figure 5.14**
Delayed trimming for $a$ :- $b(X, X), c$.

to produce with that classification. Upon private inquiry, this is what Warren proposes [War90]:

> "The general principle is that one should make variables permanent if at all possible, and use put_variable X$n$, A$i$ only as a last resort. The problem is what to do about variables which occur in only one goal. If it is the last call, one has no (real) option but to globalise the variable using put_variable X$n$, A$i$. If it is other than the last call, then one can either globalise the variable in the same way, *or* avoid trimming the variable at the immediately following call, but rather trim it at the next call, by which time it is certainly safe to do so (provided variable-variable bindings always point to the 'last-to-die' variable and the variable to be trimmed is allocated as the 'first to die' in the next call)."

Warren goes on to illustrate how, for our specific example, delayed trimming would repair the code of Figure 5.13 to that of Figure 5.14 where Y1 is kept in the environment until the time when execution returns from $b/2$, at which point it is discarded.[9]

Some comments are in order regarding this fix. First, Warren's last (cryptic) parenthetical comment simply recalls the proviso that is already ensured by our variable-variable binding convention from higher to lower addresses (WAM Binding Rule 1) and the convention set up for environment trimming allocating permanent variables in the environment so as to put the "last-to-die" first (*i.e.*, at smaller addresses)—as explained in Section 5.7.

Second, one must convince one's self that delayed trimming is indeed safe so as to warrant the simpler put_value Y1, A2 instead of the expected

---

[9]This solution using delayed trimming was also pointed out to this author by Michael Hanus [Han90] who apparently figured it out for himself, probably like many others who worked out a WAM implementation.

| | | | | | |
|---|---|---|---|---|---|
| $a/0$ | : | `allocate` | % | $a$ :- | |
| | | `put_variable Y1,A1` | % | | $b(X,$ |
| | | `put_unsafe_value Y1,A2` | % | | $X$ |
| | | `call b/2,1` | % | | $),$ |
| | | `deallocate` | % | $c$ | |
| | | `execute c/0` | % | . | |

**Figure 5.15**
Useless delayed trimming for $a$ :- $b(X,X),c.$

`put_unsafe_value Y1,A2`, as prescribed for unsafe variables. For clearly, if rather than the code of Figure 5.14, we had to generate that shown in Figure 5.15, then the whole complication would be useless. Indeed, Y1 would still be globalized on the heap, with the additional penalty of the untrimmed stack slot—not to mention the run-time check. The simpler code of Figure 5.12 would thus be clearly superior. Therefore, for the code in Figure 5.14 to be of any value, it must be guaranteed that delaying trimming Y1 makes it no longer unsafe, even though it has been initialized with `put_variable Y1,A1`. Such is the case, of course, as the unsafety of Y1 would only be caused precisely by trimming it by the call to its last goal. That it is safe to trim it at the following call is clear under the proviso of our binding and stack-allocation conventions.

In view of the foregoing considerations, the reader may now understand why we did not start out with Warren's definition for variable classification. Our reasons are quite deliberate. Firstly, in the gradual construction of our partial machines, Warren's definition is unjustifiable before the environment stack or LCO are considered. Secondly, although historically, David H. D. Warren made `put_variable Xn,Ai` systematically allocate a heap cell as a patch to accommodate LCO,[10] this instruction can be justified otherwise, as we have

---

[10]He states [War89]:

"The `put_variable Xn,Ai` instruction is a kind of hack which exists only to take care of the problems of a variable that is bound to be unsafe at LCO, namely a variable which has its first occurrence in the last call and isn't otherwise bound. This special instruction should NOT be used for any other purpose.

Variables occurring only as arguments to the last goal cannot be treated as [permanent variables] since they are bound to be unsafe, and would necessarily be globalised by the `put_unsafe_value Yn,Ai` instruction if they were treated this way. To avoid this round-about approach of creating a permanent variable only to then globalise it, the `put_variable Xn,Ai` instruction is introduced, and these variables are instead treated as [temporary variables]."

indeed shown, as evolved from the simple unification machine $\mathcal{M}_0$. Lastly, we favor our *a posteriori* approach rather than Warren's since starting with a suboptimal, but simpler to understand, variable classification constitutes a greater tutorial value as it focuses the reader's attention on mechanisms that are not affected by the fine points of this issue.

In conclusion, although Warren's variable classification is historically the original definition used in the WAM as it was conceived, and can be explained as an optimization—with the need of delayed environment trimming to be correct—this author finds his own variable classification somewhat less contrived and surely much easier to justify.

## 5.10   Indexing

The three choice point manipulation instructions impose a strictly sequential search over the list of clauses making up a definition. If all the arguments of a calling predicate are unbound variables, then there is clearly no better manner to proceed. On the other hand, when some of the arguments are at least partially instantiated, that information can be used to access unifiable clause heads more directly. In the cases where the number of clauses constituting a definition is large (as is not so rarely the case for facts), this is clearly desirable. Ideally, this requires a technique for partially interleaving unification with search. Indeed, if it can be decided at the outset that a clause head will unify exclusively with a category of data, all the more selective the search code will be. On the other hand, it may be impossible in general, or very costly at best, to generate an optimal discrimination filter based on the patterns of all arguments. Fortunately, a suboptimal compromise turns out to be quite reasonable in practice. Since Prolog programmers have a natural tendency to write code in a data structure-directed manner using discriminating patterns as first argument, it is quite acceptable to limit indexing to key on the first argument only. The WAM uses this idea as a basis for optimizing clause selection. Naturally, this applies only to procedure definitions that contain more than one clauses. In what follows, we refer to a clause head's first argument as its (indexing) key.

First, note that any clause head whose key is a variable creates a search bottleneck in a procedure definition in which it appears. Indeed, that key will unify with anything and thus its clause must be explored in all cases. For this reason, a procedure $p$ defined by the sequence of clauses $C_1, \ldots, C_n$ is partitioned as a sequence of subsequences $S_1, \ldots, S_m$, where each $S_i$ is either a *single* clause with a variable key, or a *maximal* subsequence of contiguous clauses whose keys are not variables. For example, the following definition is partitioned into the four subsequences $S_1$, $S_2$, $S_3$, and $S_4$, as shown:[11]

$$
S_1 \begin{cases}
call(XorY) :- call(X). \\
call(trace) :- trace. \\
call(XorY) :- call(Y). \\
call(notrace) :- notrace. \\
call(nl) :- nl.
\end{cases}
$$

$S_2 \quad \{ \quad call(X) :- builtin(X).$

$S_3 \quad \{ \quad call(X) :- extern(X).$

$$
S_4 \begin{cases}
call(call(X)) :- call(X). \\
call(repeat). \\
call(repeat) :- call(repeat). \\
call(true).
\end{cases}
$$

As expected, the general translating scheme for a procedure $p$ with a definition thus partitioned into subsequences $S_1, \ldots, S_m$, where $m > 1$, is:

$$
\begin{array}{lll}
p & : & \texttt{try\_me\_else } S_2 \\
  &   & \textit{code for subsequence } S_1 \\
S_2 & : & \texttt{retry\_me\_else } S_3 \\
  &   & \textit{code for subsequence } S_2 \\
  &   & \vdots \\
S_m & : & \texttt{trust\_me} \\
  &   & \textit{code for subsequence } S_m
\end{array}
$$

where `retry_me_else` is necessary only if $m > 2$. If $m = 1$, none of the above is needed and the translation boils down only to the code necessary for the single subsequence chunk. Furthermore, the simpler case where the subsequence is reduced to a single variable-key clause degenerates into the expected simpler translation pattern requiring nothing more than we had before. Thus, the code for $call/1$ above looks like:

---

[11] This example is a slight modification of that given in [War83]. The (admittedly silly) splitting of the two $or/2$ clauses is only to illustrate that this will not affect performance thanks to indexing.

| $call/1$ | : | try_me_else $S_2$ | % | |
| | | *indexed code for $S_1$* | % | |
| $S_2$ | : | retry_me_else $S_3$ | % | $call(X)$ |
| | | execute *builtin*/1 | % | $:- builtin(X).$ |
| $S_3$ | : | retry_me_else $S_4$ | % | $call(X)$ |
| | | execute *extern*/1 | % | $:- extern(X).$ |
| $S_4$ | : | trust_me | % | |
| | | *indexed code for $S_4$* | % | |

Let us then focus on indexing within a non variable-key subsequence.

The technique of clause indexing for a subsequence uses one or two levels of dispatching according to the run-time sort of the calling procedure's first argument, and possibly a third level consisting of sequential threading together some preselected clauses. A first level of dispatching is performed depending on whether the dereferenced value of A1 is a variable, a constant, a (non-empty) list, or a general structure. In each case, control is to jump to a (possibly void) bucket of clauses. Respectively, the code bucket of a variable corresponds to full sequential search through the subsequence (thus, it is never void), that of a constant (resp., of a structure) corresponds to a further dispatching level discriminating among different constants (resp., different structures), and that of a list corresponds either to the single clause with a list key or to a linked list of all those clauses in the subsequence whose keys are lists. For those constants (or structures) having multiple clauses, a possible third level bucket corresponds to the linked list of these clauses (just like the possible second level for lists).

Hence, the general indexing code pattern for a subsequence is of the form:

*first level indexing;*
*second level indexing;*
*third level indexing;*
*code of clauses in subsequence order;*

where second and third levels are only necessary as dictated by what sort of keys are present in the subsequence and in what number. In particular, they may be altogether eliminated as appropriate in the degenerate cases. The last part following the dispatching code is simply the regular sequential choice control construction. For example, the subsequence $S_1$ of $call/1$ is translated thus:

*first level indexing for* $S_1$
*second level indexing for* $S_1$
*third level indexing for* $S_1$

$S_{11}$ : try_me_else $S_{12}$
*code for 'call*($X$ *or* $Y$) : $-$ *call*($X$).'

$S_{12}$ : retry_me_else $S_{13}$
*code for 'call*(*trace*) : $-$ *trace*.'

$S_{13}$ : retry_me_else $S_{14}$
*code for 'call*($X$ *or* $Y$) : $-$ *call*($Y$).'

$S_{14}$ : retry_me_else $S_{15}$
*code for 'call*(*notrace*) : $-$ *notrace*.'

$S_{15}$ : trust_me
*code for 'call*(*nl*) : $-$ *nl*.'

Therefore, we need instructions for each dispatching level in the general case.

First level dispatching is done with the switch_on_term $V, C, L, S$ instruction whose effect is to make control jump to the instruction labeled, respectively, $V$, $C$, $L$, or $S$, depending on whether the dereferenced value of A1 is a variable, a constant, a non-empty list, or a structure, respectively.

Second level dispatching for $N$ distinct constants (having realized that A1 dereferences to one) is done with switch_on_constant $N, T$, where $T$ is a hash-table of size $N$ of the form $\{c_i : L_{c_i}\}_{i=1}^{N}$ associating to each distinct constant $c_i$ used as a key in the subsequence a label $L_{c_i}$ where control must jump when $c_i$ is passed as first argument. If the constant found in A1 is not one in the table, backtracking occurs. The similar instruction switch_on_structure $N, T$ does the same for all distinct (non-constant non-list) functors in the subsequence. Second level list indexing is really third level indexing on list structures, the second level being skipped by special handling of lists in the spirit of WAM Principle 3.

Third level indexing corresponds to threading together multiple (but not necessarily contiguous) clauses whose keys are lists, or a same constant or structure. Since the code of all clauses in the subsequence are already so-threaded by a try_me_else, (retry_me_else) trust_me choice control construction, its clause code subsequence relevant only to the recognized key at hand (be it list, constant, or structure) must be accessed explicitly with an alternative choice control construction. This is achieved by using three instructions, try $L$, retry $L$, trust $L$. These are almost identical to try_me_else $L$, retry_me_else $L$, and trust_me, respectively. The only difference is that they use the specified label $L$ for the instruction to jump to, saving the next one in sequence as the next clause alternative in the choice point (except for trust, of course).

The complete indexing code for subsequence $S_1$ of the *call*/1 example is given in Figure 5.16, and that for subsequence $S_4$ is given in Figure 5.17. The complete indexing code for *call*/1 can thus be patched together from these and the partitioned scheme for $S_1$, $S_2$, $S_3$, and $S_4$ given earlier. An illustration of a degenerate case where all three levels of indexing are not necessary is given in Figure 5.18 for the familiar *conc* definition for concatenating two lists:

$conc([], L, L).$
$conc([H|T], L, [H|R]) :- conc(T, L, R).$

It is interesting to observe that when the *conc*/3 procedure is called with an instantiated first argument, no choice point frame for it is ever needed. As a matter of fact, using indexing has a major incidental benefit as it substantially reduces the creation and manipulation of choice point frames on the stack. This has as corollary that it also reduces the effects of environment protection, and thus magnifies the gain of LCO and environment trimming. For example, let us assume that a list processing procedure *lp* is defined as:

$lp([H|T]) :- process(H), lp(T).$
$lp([]).$

Some programmers have indeed taken the habit of specifying the []-clause last using Prolog interpreters. They reason that since there are many more [_|_]'s in a list than the single final [], this procedure, when invoked with an instantiated first argument, will backtrack only once at the end of list before reaching initial success. However, with a compiler using LCO but no clause indexing, this will annihilate all effects of LCO because a choice point will systematically cover every recursive call's environment to *lp* with a non-empty list in the key position. Whereas, for such calls clause indexing will eliminate all choice points and transform either ordering of the two clauses into fast iterative code.

All explicit definitions for the indexing instructions are given in Appendix B.

**Exercise 5.4** The effect of the switch_on_constant instruction described above is that given originally by Warren in [War83]. However, it does useless work as it eventually leads to a get_constant instruction that redundantly tests whether register A1 contains that very same constant that was seen in A1 by switch_on_constant. Can you propose a simple optimization to avoid this redundancy? [*Hint: Beware of intermediate levels of indexing.*]

```
          switch_on_term S₁₁, C₁, fail, F₁        % 1st level dispatch for S₁
```

$C_1$  :  `switch_on_constant 3,{` *trace*    `:` $S_{1b}$,       % *2nd level for constants*
                                   *notrace* `:` $S_{1d}$,
                                   *nl*       `:` $S_{1e}$ `}`

$F_1$  :  `switch_on_structure 1,{` *or*/2 `:` $F_{11}$ `}`     % *2nd level for structures*

$F_{11}$ :  `try` $S_{1a}$                                     % *3rd level for or*/2
            `trust` $S_{1c}$                                   %

$S_{11}$ :  `try_me_else` $S_{12}$                             % *call*
$S_{1a}$ :  `get_structure` *or*/2, A1                         %      (*or*
            `unify_variable` A1                                %        (*X*,
            `unify_void` 1                                     %           *Y*))
            `execute` *call*/1                                 %      :− *call*(*X*).

$S_{12}$ :  `retry_me_else` $S_{13}$                           % *call*
$S_{1b}$ :  `get_constant` *trace*, A1                         %      (*trace*)
            `execute` *trace*/0                                %      :− *trace*.

$S_{13}$ :  `retry_me_else` $S_{14}$                           % *call*
$S_{1c}$ :  `get_structure` *or*/2, A1                         %      (*or*
            `unify_void` 1                                     %        (*X*,
            `unify_variable` A1                                %           *Y*))
            `execute` *call*/1                                 %      :− *call*(*Y*).

$S_{14}$ :  `retry_me_else` $S_{15}$                           % *call*
$S_{1d}$ :  `get_constant` *notrace*, A1                       %      (*notrace*)
            `execute` *notrace*/0                              %      :− *notrace*.

$S_{15}$ :  `trust_me`                                         % *call*
$S_{1e}$ :  `get_constant` *nl*, A1                            %      (*nl*)
            `execute` *nl*/0                                   %      :− *nl*.
```

**Figure 5.16**

Indexing code for subsequence $S_1$
```

| $S_4$ | | switch_on_term $S_{41}, C_4, \mathit{fail}, F_4$ | % | 1st level dispatch for $S_4$ |
|---|---|---|---|---|
| $C_4$ | : | switch_on_constant 3, { *repeat* : $C_{41}$, | % | 2nd level for constants |
| | | *true* : $S_{4d}$ } | | |
| $F_4$ | : | switch_on_structure 1, { *call*/1 : $S_{41}$ } | % | 2nd level for structures |
| $C_{41}$ | : | try $S_{4b}$ | % | 3rd level for 'repeat' |
| | | trust $S_{4c}$ | % | |
| $S_{41}$ | : | try_me_else $S_{42}$ | % | *call* |
| $S_{4a}$ | : | get_structure *call*/1, A1 | % | (*call* |
| | | unify_variable A1 | % | ($X$)) |
| | | execute *call*/1 | % | :- *call*($X$). |
| $S_{42}$ | : | retry_me_else $S_{43}$ | % | *call* |
| $S_{4b}$ | : | get_constant *repeat*, A1 | % | (*repeat*) |
| | | proceed | % | . |
| $S_{43}$ | : | retry_me_else $S_{44}$ | % | *call* |
| $S_{4c}$ | : | get_constant *repeat*, A1 | % | (*repeat*) |
| | | put_constant *repeat*, A1 | % | :- *call*(*repeat*) |
| | | execute *call*/1 | % | . |
| $S_{44}$ | : | trust_me | % | *call* |
| $S_{4d}$ | : | get_constant *true*, A1 | % | (*true*) |
| | | proceed | % | . |

**Figure 5.17**
Indexing code for subsequence $S_4$

| | | | | |
|---|---|---|---|---|
| $conc/3$ | : | switch_on_term $C_{1a}, C_1, C_2, fail$ | % | |
| $C_{1a}$ | : | try_me_else $C_{2a}$ | % | *conc* |
| $C_1$ | : | get_constant [], A1 | % | ([], |
| | | get_value A2, A3 | % | $L, L)$ |
| | | proceed | % | |
| $C_{2a}$ | : | trust_me | % | *conc* |
| $C_2$ | : | get_list A1 | % | ([ |
| | | unify_variable X4 | % | $H\|$ |
| | | unify_variable A1 | % | $T], L,$ |
| | | get_list A3 | % | [ |
| | | unify_value X4 | % | $H\|$ |
| | | unify_variable A3 | % | $R])$ |
| | | execute $conc/3$ | % | $:- conc(T, L, R).$ |

**Figure 5.18**
Encoding of *conc*/3

**Exercise 5.5** If you could figure out a solution for Exercise 5.4, can it also
work or be adapted to avoid a redundant A1 check by get_structure after
switch_on_structure? [*Hint: Beware of the setting of the* S *register and
that of* read/write *mode.*]

## 5.11  Cut

In this last section, we explain how the design obtained after the compounding
of all the foregoing optimizations can be augmented to accommodate implementation of the Prolog cut. The treatment of cut was not part of the original
WAM report [War83]. The material we present here is extrapolated from what
was sketched in [War88] and suggestions from Dean Rosenzweig [Ros91].

As is well-known, the cut predicate (noted '!') is an extra-logical control
annotation that helps the Prolog programmer trim the search space. The
operational semantics of '!' is simply to succeed with a side effect on
backtracking information; namely, once passed, it makes control forget any
other potential alternative for the procedure in whose clause it appears as well
as any other arising from preceding body goals.

In terms of the machine architecture at hand, this effect is obtained by discarding all choice point frames that were created after the choice point frame that was current right before the call of the procedure containing the cut. Let us assume that the appropriate choice point where to return upon backtracking over a cut is maintained in a global register called the *cut register* and noted B0. Clearly, the value of B0 must be set to the address of the choice point that is current at the time a procedure call is made. This is achieved by altering the call and execute instructions to set B0 to the value of the current value of B. In this way, executing a cut amounts essentially to resetting B to the value of B0.

There are really two sorts of cuts to consider: *shallow* and *deep* cuts. A shallow cut is one located between the head and the body of the rule immediately after the ' : - ' symbol (thus also called *neck cut*—somewhat euphemistically), as in:

$$h :- !, b_1, \ldots, b_n.$$

while a deep cut is any other, of the form:

$$h :- \ldots, b_i, !, \ldots, b_n. \quad (1 \leq i \leq n).$$

Before looking at each case in detail, let us first make an important observation regarding the creation of choice points. While it is easy to see that clause indexing may bypass creating a choice point for a multiple-clause procedure, it is perhaps less immediate to realize that indexing may also cause creating *an additional choice point* for such a procedure. For instance, refer to the *call*/1 procedure given on Page 66. Its instruction sequence (Page 67) starts with:

$$call/1 : \text{try\_me\_else } S_2$$

which creates one choice point for *call*/1. Further down in that procedure's instruction sequence, what constitutes subsequence $S_1$ (given as Figure 5.16 on Page 70) contains the instruction:

$$F_{11} : \text{try } S_{1a}$$

that will create a second choice point for *call*/1 if executed.[12]

Let us first consider the simpler case where the clause containing the cut, be it shallow or deep, is the first (not necessarily in sequence thanks to

---

[12]This fact was brought to our attention by Dean Rosenzweig [Ros91] who noticed that the scheme given in [AK90] was erroneous. We gratefully acknowledge his suggesting the corrected scheme we describe next.

indexing) among those of the called procedure's to be executed upon entering the procedure with `call` or `execute`. We shall see later what to do in the other case where backtracking occurred since the original call.

Upon starting executing the instruction sequence of the clause containing a shallow cut, B0 is either equal to B (since indexing could have bypassed creating a choice point for the procedure containing the rule), or equal to one of the two previous choice points preceding B. If B0 and B are equal, there is no action to be taken by the cut since this call does not have alternatives anyway. Otherwise (B > B0), the shallow cut must discard any (one or two) choice points following B. This action is the same in either case (*i.e.*, B ← B0, HB ← B.H). This is the main effect of the new instruction `neck_cut` into which a shallow cut occurrence is translated. For instance, the body of:

$$a :- !, b.$$

is compiled into:

```
neck_cut
execute b/0
```

The resetting of B and HB is not quite all that may be done upon a cut. Indeed, discarding a choice point may change the status of some bindings recorded as conditional in the trail which will have become unconditional for those heap (resp., stack) variables whose addresses will now be greater than HB (resp., B). Therefore, this calls for a clean-up of the trail up to the trail address indicated by the reinstated choice point frame. This amounts to removing the appropriate addresses from the trail and tamping it down to eliminate the holes this may have created in it. (This operation is given as an ancillary operation called *tidy_trail* in Appendix B.)

Regarding deep cuts, the complication is that the calls to intervening body goals will overwrite the cut register B0 between the time the clause containing the cut in entered and the time the cut is executed. However, all choice points created between the setting of B0 upon calling this clause's procedure and this deep cut must be discarded. Therefore, in exactly the same way as for CP, it will be necessary to save B0 further as part of the cut clause's environment. Fortunately, it is not necessary to do so systematically for all clauses since most do not contain deep cuts. Thus, rather than extending the format of an environment frame with a special slot for B0 as we did for CP, it is preferable to save it as a pseudo permanent variable. The situation then is to assimilate a deep cut occurrence as !($Y$), where $Y$ is a permanent variable distinct from all other variables in the clause. This variable is allocated in the current environment to accommodate environment trimming just like the other real permanent variables (*i.e.*, its offset is greater than the subsequent goal's and less that the preceding goal's). With this, we only need two new instructions:

(1)  `get_level` Y$n$
(2)  `cut` Y$n$

such that (1) `get_level` Y$n$ always appear immediately after `allocate` in the clause, having for effect to set Y$n$ to contain the current value of B0; whereas, (2) `cut` Y$n$ discards all (if any) choice points after that indicated by Y$n$, and cleans up new unconditional bindings from the trail up to that point. For example,

$a :- b, !, c.$

is compiled into:

```
allocate
get_level Y1
call b/0, 1
cut Y1
deallocate
execute c/0
```

Note now that the presence of a deep cut in a rule that would otherwise be a chain rule (*e.g.*, $a :- b, !$.) makes it a deep rule requiring environment allocation. However, this not the case when a shallow cut occurs in rule that would otherwise be a chain rule. A neck cut does not make such a rule a deep rule, even though it might be construed as having two body goals.

The scheme just described deals correctly with cuts in the case where the clause in question is the first executed among those of the called procedure. However, it is not quite complete as given to be correct if the clause is executed after backtracking within the same procedure. Then, there is yet the problem of restoring a correct value for B0. For example, consider the following pattern:

$a :- b, c.$
$a :- !, d.$
$a :- \ldots$

At the time $a$ is called, B0 is set to the current choice point. When the clause $a :- b, c.$ is executed, the call to $b$ overwrites B0. Now, if the call to $b$ fails, backtracking to the following clause will execute the shallow cut and reset B to the spurious value left in B0 by the failed call to *b*.

This simple example illustrates the need for restoring B0 to a correct value upon backtracking. But what (and where) is this correct value? It would *not* be correct to reset B0 to the choice point preceding the current B since, as observed before, indexing may have created two choice points for the procedure and there is no simple way to detect this. The solution that we adopt here is simple. (More efficient but more complicated alternatives can be devised—*e.g.*, see Exercise 5.6.) Namely, the value of the cut register B0 is systematically saved as part of a choice point at its creation and restored upon backtracking from that information saved in the current choice point. Accordingly, the format of a choice point frame given on Page 32 is extended with an additional slot for this purpose (as shown in the complete layout on Page 104) and the try_me_else and try instructions are modified appropriately. (So is allocate since it must account for this additional slot space when B is the top of the stack.)

We now have a complete and correct scheme for handling cut. All the machinery we just presented is taken into account in the explicit definitions of the complete WAM instructions given in Appendix B.

> **Exercise 5.6** The following is suggested by [Ros91]. The problem of knowing to which value B0 must be restored upon backtracking may be solved in a better way than systematically saving it as part of a choice point. It is possible to use two slightly different versions for retry_me_else (resp., retry) depending on the level of indexing they are used for. An "outer" version, say retry_me_else_1 (resp., retry_1) would reset B0 to the previous choice point, and an inner version , say retry_me_else_2 (resp., retry_2) would reset B0 to the choice point preceding the previous one. Give a correct translation scheme and all appropriate modifications needed in the explicit definitions of Appendix B to implement this solution.

> **Exercise 5.7** Refer to the remark made in Footnote 3 on Page 31. Give all appropriate modifications needed in the pseudo-code given in Appendix B defining the WAM instructions and ancillary operations in order to eliminate the arity slot from choice point frames.

# 6 Conclusion

In this tutorial, we have conducted an exhaustive reconstruction of an abstract machine architecture for Prolog as completely as it has been conceived by David H. D. Warren. Starting from a mere first-order term unification machine, we have elaborated its design gradually, introducing each needed concept as didactically as we thought possible. Doing so, we have striven to justify every single design decision, explicating often subtle interplays as they arose.

Obviously, the design that we have attained necessarily does not contain all the tools needed for constructing a complete Prolog compiler and run-time environment. Namely, many details regarding other interesting Prolog control constructs (*e.g.*, conditional, freeze, *etc.*), extra-logical and built-in procedures (*e.g.*, assert/retract, setof, *etc.*), input/output facilities, *etc.*, are yet to be spelled out. However, all this is clearly beyond the scope of this tutorial. These additional features, as well as any other operationally well-defined interesting extensions, can be integrated into the pure WAM design we have presented without excessive labor.

For those interested in more advanced material using WAM ideas, some works are worth mentioning for further reading. In particular, the manner in which the WAM regards unification has a strong relation with partial evaluation techniques as explained in particular in [Kur87]. Also, since compilation as done by the WAM treats each procedure independently of the rest of the program, global analysis techniques can therefore be considered as in [Mel85, DW86a, DW86b, Deb89, DW89, vR90, vRD90]. Finally, one will find copious material about improving backtracking in Prolog in [PP82, BP84, Cox84, CCF88, ZTU90, Zho90].

At any rate, we hope to have contributed to give the reader a rapid and clear understanding with thorough, if not formal, justification of all the details of the essential abstract machine. Our aim has been to leave as little unexplained as possible, opening up Warren's original design. Seen thus decomposed and reconstructed from its logical components, the WAM's organization and workings lose all mystery. Yet, far from lessening its designer's credit, understanding the WAM can make one appreciate all the more David H. D. Warren's feat, as he conceived this architecture in his mind as one whole. We are pleased to have shared with the reader our admiration for his contribution's adequacy and elegance.

# A Prolog in a Nutshell

We first present basic notions for first-order terms and substitutions. Then, we describe a non-deterministic unification algorithm as a set of solution-preserving transformations on a set of equations due to Herbrand [Her71] (*cf.*, Page 148) and rediscovered by Martelli-Montanari [MM82]. Then, we summarize the essence of Prolog's operational semantics.

## Terms and substitutions

Let $\{\Sigma_n\}_{n \geq 0}$ be an indexed family of mutually disjoint sets of (function) symbols of arity $n$. Let $\Sigma = \bigcup_{n \geq 0} \Sigma_n$ be the set of all function symbols. Let $\mathcal{V}$ be a countably infinite set of *variables*. By convention, variables will be capitalized not to confuse them with constants in $\Sigma_0$.

Let $\mathcal{T}$ be the set of (first-order) *terms* defined as the smallest set such that:

- if $X \in \mathcal{V}$ then $X \in \mathcal{T}$;
- if $a \in \Sigma_0$ then $a \in \mathcal{T}$;
- if $f \in \Sigma_n$, $(n \geq 1)$, and $t_i \in \mathcal{T}, (1 \leq i \leq n)$, then $f(t_1, \ldots, t_n) \in \mathcal{T}$.

For example, given the signature $\Sigma$ such that $p \in \Sigma_3$, $h \in \Sigma_2$, $f \in \Sigma_1$, and $a \in \Sigma_0$, and given that $W$, $X$, $Y$, and $Z$ are variables in $\mathcal{V}$, the terms $p(Z, h(Z, W), f(W))$ and $p(f(X), h(Y, f(a)), Y)$ are in $\mathcal{T}$.

A *substitution* is a finitely non-identical assignment of terms to variables; *i.e.*, a function $\sigma$ from $\mathcal{V}$ to $\mathcal{T}$ such that the set $\{X \in \mathcal{V} \mid X \neq \sigma(X)\}$ is finite. This set is called the *domain* of $\sigma$ and denoted by $\mathbf{dom}(\sigma)$. Such a substitution is also written as a set such as $\sigma = \{t_i/X_i\}_{i=1}^n$ where $\mathbf{dom}(\sigma) = \{X_i\}_{i=1}^n$ and $\sigma(X_i) = t_i$ for $i = 1$ to $n$.

A substitution $\sigma$ is uniquely extended to a function $\overline{\sigma}$ from $\mathcal{T}$ to $\mathcal{T}$ as follows:

- $\overline{\sigma}(X) = \sigma(X)$, if $X \in \mathcal{V}$;
- $\overline{\sigma}(a) = a$, if $a \in \Sigma_0$;
- $\overline{\sigma}(f(t_1, \ldots, t_n)) = f(\overline{\sigma}(t_1), \ldots, \overline{\sigma}(t_n))$, if $f \in \Sigma_n, t_i \in \mathcal{T}, (1 \leq i \leq n)$.

Since they coincide on $\mathcal{V}$, and for notation convenience, we deliberately confuse a substitution $\sigma$ and its extension $\overline{\sigma}$. Also, rather than writing $\sigma(t)$, we shall write $t\sigma$. Given two substitutions $\sigma = \{t_i/X_i\}_{i=1}^n$ and $\theta = \{s_j/Y_j\}_{j=1}^m$, their composition $\sigma\theta$ is the substitution which yields the same result on all terms as first applying $\sigma$ then applying $\theta$ on the result. One computes such a composition as the set:

$$\sigma\theta = ( \{t\theta/X \mid t/X \in \sigma\} - \{X/X \mid X \in \textbf{dom}(\sigma)\} )$$
$$\cup ( \theta - \{s/Y \mid Y \in \textbf{dom}(\sigma)\} ).$$

For example, if $\sigma = \{f(Y)/X, U/V\}$ and $\theta = \{b/X, f(a)/Y, V/U\}$, then composing $\sigma$ and $\theta$ yields $\sigma\theta = \{f(f(a))/X, f(a)/Y, V/U\}$, while composing $\theta$ and $\sigma$ gives $\theta\sigma = \{b/X, f(a)/Y, U/V\}$.

Composition defines a preorder (*i.e.*, a reflexive and transitive relation) on substitutions. A substitution $\sigma$ is *more general* than a substitution $\theta$ iff there exists a substitution $\rho$ such that $\theta = \sigma\rho$. For example, $\{f(Y)/X\}$ is more general than $\{f(f(a))/X, f(a)/Y\}$.

## Unification algorithm

An *equation* is a pair of terms, written $s = t$. A substitution $\sigma$ is a *solution* (or a *unifier*) of a set of equations $\{s_i = t_i\}_{i=1}^n$ iff $s_i\sigma = t_i\sigma$ for all $i = 1, \ldots, n$. Two sets of equations are *equivalent* iff they both admit *all* and *only* the same solutions. Following [MM82], we define two transformations on sets of equations—*term decomposition* and *variable elimination*. They both preserve solutions of sets of equations.

> **Term Decomposition** *If a set $E$ of equations contains an equation of the form $f(s_1, \ldots, s_n) = f(t_1, \ldots, t_n)$, where $f \in \Sigma_n, (n \geq 0)$, then the set $E' = E - \{f(s_1, \ldots, s_n) = f(t_1, \ldots, t_n)\} \cup \{s_i = t_i\}_{i=1}^n$ is equivalent to $E$.*[1]

> **Variable Elimination** *If a set $E$ of equations contains an equation of the form $X = t$ where $t \neq X$, then the set $E' = (E - \{X = t\})\sigma \cup \{X = t\}$ where $\sigma = \{t/X\}$, is equivalent to $E$.*

A set of equations $E$ is partitioned into two subsets: its *solved* part and its *unsolved* part. The solved part is its maximal subset of equations of the form $X = t$ such that $X$ occurs nowhere in the full set of equations except as the left-hand side of this equation alone. The unsolved part is the complement of the solved part. A set of equations is said to be *fully solved* iff its unsolved part is empty.

Following is a unification algorithm. It is a non-deterministic normalization procedure for a given set $E$ of equations which repeatedly chooses and performs one of the following transformations until none applies or failure is encountered.

---

[1] If $n = 0$, the equation is simply deleted.

($u$.1) Select any equation of the form $t = X$ where $t$ is not a variable, and rewrite it as $X = t$.

($u$.2) Select any equation of the form $X = X$ and erase it.

($u$.3) Select any equation of the form $f(s_1, \ldots, s_n) = g(t_1, \ldots, t_m)$ where $f \in \Sigma_n$ and $g \in \Sigma_m$, $(n, m \geq 0)$; if $f \neq g$ or $n \neq m$, stop with failure; otherwise, if $n = 0$ erase the equation, else $(n \geq 1)$ replace it with $n$ equations $s_i = t_i$, $(i = 1, \ldots, n)$.

($u$.4) Select any equation of the form $X = t$ where $X$ is a variable which occurs somewhere else in the set of equations and such that $t \neq X$. If $t$ is of the form $f(t_1, \ldots, t_n)$, where $f \in \Sigma_n$, and if $X$ occurs in $t$, then stop with failure; otherwise, let $\sigma = \{t/X\}$ and replace every other equation $l = r$ by $l\sigma = r\sigma$.

If this procedure terminates with success, the set of equations which emerges as the outcome is fully solved. Its solved part defines a substitution called the *most general unifier* (MGU) of all the terms participating as sides of equations in $E$. If it terminates with failure, the set of equations $E$ is unsatisfiable and no unifier for it exists.

The set $E = \{p(Z, h(Z, W), f(W)) = p(f(X), h(Y, f(a)), Y)\}$, for example, is normalized as follows:

$\{Z = f(X) , h(Z, W) = h(Y, f(a)) , f(W) = Y\}$          [by ($u$.3)]

$\{Z = f(X) , h(f(X), W) = h(Y, f(a)) , f(W) = Y\}$          [by ($u$.4)]

$\{Z = f(X) , f(X) = Y , W = f(a) , f(W) = Y\}$          [by ($u$.3)]

$\{Z = f(X) , Y = f(X) , W = f(a) , f(W) = Y\}$          [by ($u$.1)]

$\{Z = f(X) , Y = f(X) , W = f(a) , f(W) = f(X)\}$          [by ($u$.4)]

$\{Z = f(X) , Y = f(X) , W = f(a) , f(f(a)) = f(X)\}$          [by ($u$.4)]

$\{Z = f(X) , Y = f(X) , W = f(a) , f(a) = X\}$          [by ($u$.3)]

$\{Z = f(X) , Y = f(X) , W = f(a) , X = f(a)\}$          [by ($u$.1)]

$\{Z = f(f(a)) , Y = f(f(a)) , W = f(a) , X = f(a)\}$          [by ($u$.4)]

producing the substitution $\sigma = \{f(f(a))/Z, f(a)/W, f(f(a))/Y, f(a)/X\}$ which is the MGU of $p(Z, h(Z, W), f(W))$ and $p(f(X), h(Y, f(a)), Y)$ and both yield the same term $p(f(f(a)), h(f(f(a)), f(a)), f(f(a)))$ when applied the substitution $\sigma$.

## Prolog

Logic programming, of which Prolog is *the* canonical language, expresses programs as relational rules of the form:

$$r_0(\vec{t_0}) :- r_1(\vec{t_1}), \ldots, r_n(\vec{t_n}).$$

where the $r_i$'s are relationals symbols and the $\vec{t_i}$'s are tuples of first-order terms. One reads such a rule as: *"For all bindings of their variables, the terms $\vec{t_0}$ are in relation $r_0$ if the terms $\vec{t_1}$ are in relation $r_1$ and ... the terms $\vec{t_n}$ are in relation $r_n$."* In the case where $n = 0$, the rule reduces to the simple unconditional assertion, or *fact*, $r_0(\vec{t_0})$ that the terms $\vec{t_0}$ are in relation $r_0$. A fact will be written omitting the $:-$ symbol. These rules are called *definite clauses*; expressions such as $r_i(\vec{t_i})$ are called *atoms*; the *head* of a definite clause is the atom on the left of the $:-$ symbol, and its *body* is the conjunction of atoms on its right.

For example, the following are two definite clauses, the first one being a fact:

$conc([], L, L).$
$conc(H.T, L, H.R) :- conc(T, L, R).$

where '$[]$' $\in \Sigma_0$ is a constant and the function symbol '$.$' $\in \Sigma_2$ is written in infix notation. This may be used as a program to concatenate two lists where $[]$ is used as a list terminator.[2]

A *query* is a clause of the form:

$$:- q_1(\vec{s_1}), \ldots, q_m(\vec{s_m}).$$

A query as shown above may be read: *"Does there exist some binding of variables such that the terms $\vec{s_1}$ are in relation $q_1$ and ... $\vec{s_m}$ are in relation $q_m$?"* To emphasize that this is interpreted as a question, the symbol $:-$ is then written $?-$ as in:

$$?- q_1(\vec{s_1}), \ldots, q_m(\vec{s_m}).$$

SLD resolution is a non-deterministic deduction rule by which queries are transformed. It owes its origins to Automatic Theorem Proving based on the Resolution Principle discovered by J. A. Robinson [Rob65] and was

---

[2]For example, 1.2.3.[] is a list. Edinburgh Prolog syntax uses $[X|Y]$ instead of $X.Y$; it also uses a simplified variant to express a list *in extenso*, allowing writing [1,2,3] rather than $[1|[2|[3|[]]]]$.

proposed by R. A. Kowalski [Kow79] as a computation rule. Technically, it is characterized as linear resolution over definite clauses, using a selection function. Linear resolution is a particular restriction of the non-deterministic application of the general deduction rule defined in [Rob65] so that one single fixed clause keeps being transformed by resolving it against other clauses in a given set. SLD resolution is a further restriction of linear resolution where (1) the fixed clause is a query, (2) clauses in the set are definite, and (3) an oracular function selects which atom in the query to resolve on and which definite clause in the set to resolve against. Thus, the letters "SLD" stand respectively for "*Selection*," "*Linear*," and "*Definite*."

More specifically, using the above Prolog notation for queries and rules, SLD resolution consists in choosing an atom $q_i(\vec{s_i})$ in the query's body and a definite clause in the given set whose head $r_0(\vec{t_0})$ *unifies* with $q_i(\vec{s_i})$ thanks to a variable substitution $\sigma$ (*i.e.*, $q_i(\vec{s_i})\sigma = r_0(\vec{t_0})\sigma$), then replacing it by the body of that clause in the query, applying substitution $\sigma$ to all the new query. That is,

$$?- q_1(\vec{s_1})\sigma, \ldots, q_{i-1}(\vec{s_{i-1}})\sigma, r_1(\vec{t_1})\sigma, \ldots, r_n(\vec{t_n})\sigma, q_{i+1}(\vec{s_{i+1}})\sigma, \ldots, q_m(\vec{s_m})\sigma.$$

The process is repeated and stops when and if the query's body is empty (success) or no rule head unifies with the selected atom (failure). There are two non-deterministic choices made in the process: one of an atom to rewrite in the query and one among the potentially many rules whose head to unify with this atom. In any case, SLD resolution is *sound* (*i.e.*, it does not derive wrong solutions) and, provided these choices are made by a fair non-deterministic selection function, it is also *complete* (*i.e.*, it derives all solutions).

Prolog's computation rule is a particular deterministic approximation of SLD resolution. Specifically, it is a flattening of SLD resolution emulating a depth-first search. It sees a program as an *ordered* set of definite clauses, and a query or definite clause body as an *ordered* set of atoms. These orders are meant to provide a rigid guide for the two choices made by the selection function of SLD resolution. Thus, Prolog's particular computation strategy transforms a query by rewriting the query attempting to unify its leftmost atom with the head of the first rule according to the order in which they are specified. If failure is encountered, a backtracking step to the latest rule choice point is made, and computation resumed there with the next alternative given by the following rule. For example, if the two clauses for predicate *conc* are given as above, then the Prolog query '$?- conc(1.2.T, 3.4.[], L).$' succeeds with the substitution $T = [], L = 1.2.3.4.[]$, while the query '$?- conc(1.2.[], X, 3.Y).$' fails.

Strategies for choice of where to apply linear resolution are all logically consistent in the sense that if computation terminates, the variable binding exhibited is a legitimate solution to the original query. In particular, like non-deterministic SLD resolution, Prolog resolution is *sound*. However, unlike non-deterministic SLD resolution, it is *incomplete*. Indeed, Prolog's particular strategy of doing linear resolution may diverge although finitely derivable solutions to a query may exist. For example, if the definite clauses for *conc* are given in a different order (*i.e.*, first the rule, then the fact), then the query '$?- conc(X, Y, Z)$.' never terminates although it has (infinitely many) finitely derivable solutions!

# B The WAM at a glance

## B.1 WAM instructions

We summarize here for quick reference all the instructions of the WAM. In some instructions, we use the notation $Vn$ to denote a variable that may be indifferently temporary or permanent.

### The complete set:

**Put instructions**

```
put_variable Xn, Ai
put_variable Yn, Ai
put_value Vn, Ai
put_unsafe_value Yn, Ai
put_structure f, Ai
put_list Ai
put_constant c, Ai
```

**Get instructions**

```
get_variable Vn, Ai
get_value Vn, Ai
get_structure f, Ai
get_list Ai
get_constant c, Ai
```

**Set instructions**

```
set_variable Vn
set_value Vn
set_local_value Vn
set_constant c
set_void n
```

**Unify instructions**

```
unify_variable Vn
unify_value Vn
unify_local_value Vn
unify_constant c
unify_void n
```

**Control instructions**

```
allocate
deallocate
call P, N
execute P
proceed
```

**Choice instructions**

```
try_me_else L
retry_me_else L
trust_me
try L
retry L
trust L
```

**Indexing instructions**

```
switch_on_term V, C, L, S
switch_on_constant N, T
switch_on_structure N, T
```

**Cut instructions**

```
neck_cut
get_level Yn
cut Yn
```

## Put instructions

| put_variable Xn, Ai |

Push a new unbound REF cell onto the
heap and copy it into both register Xn
and register Ai. Continue execution
with the following instruction.

$$HEAP[H] \leftarrow \langle REF, H \rangle;$$
$$Xn \leftarrow HEAP[H];$$
$$Ai \leftarrow HEAP[H];$$
$$H \leftarrow H + 1;$$
$$P \leftarrow P + instruction\_size(P);$$

| put_variable Yn, Ai |

Initialize the $n$-th stack variable in the
current environment to 'unbound' and
let Ai point to it. Continue execution
with the following instruction.

$$addr \leftarrow E + n + 1;$$
$$STACK[addr] \leftarrow \langle REF, addr \rangle;$$
$$Ai \leftarrow STACK[addr];$$
$$P \leftarrow P + instruction\_size(P);$$

| put_value Vn, Ai |

Place the contents of Vn into register Ai.
Continue execution with the following
instruction.

$$Ai \leftarrow Vn;$$
$$P \leftarrow P + instruction\_size(P);$$

| put_unsafe_value Yn, Ai |

If the dereferenced value of Yn is not
an unbound stack variable in the current environment, set Ai to that value.
Otherwise, bind the referenced stack
variable to a new unbound variable cell
pushed on the heap, and set Ai to point
to that cell. Continue execution with
the following instruction.

$$addr \leftarrow deref(E + n + 1);$$
**if** $addr < E$
   **then** $Ai \leftarrow STORE[addr]$
   **else**
     **begin**
       $HEAP[H] \leftarrow \langle REF, H \rangle;$
       $bind(addr, H);$
       $Ai \leftarrow HEAP[H];$
       $H \leftarrow H + 1$
     **end**;
$$P \leftarrow P + instruction\_size(P);$$

$\boxed{\texttt{put\_structure } f, \texttt{A}i}$

Push a new functor cell containing $f$ onto the heap and set register A$i$ to an STR cell pointing to that functor cell. Continue execution with the following instruction.

$\texttt{HEAP[H]} \leftarrow f/n;$
$\texttt{A}i \leftarrow \langle\, \texttt{STR}\,,\texttt{H}\,\rangle;$
$\texttt{H} \leftarrow \texttt{H} + 1;$
$\texttt{P} \leftarrow \texttt{P} + instruction\_size(\texttt{P});$

$\boxed{\texttt{put\_list } \texttt{A}i}$

Set register A$i$ to contain a LIS cell pointing to the current top of the heap. Continue execution with the following instruction.

$\texttt{A}i \leftarrow \langle\, \texttt{LIS}\,,\texttt{H}\,\rangle;$
$\texttt{P} \leftarrow \texttt{P} + instruction\_size(\texttt{P});$

$\boxed{\texttt{put\_constant } c, \texttt{A}i}$

Place a constant cell containing $c$ into register A$i$. Continue execution with the following instruction.

$\texttt{A}i \leftarrow \langle\, \texttt{CON}\,,c\,\rangle;$
$\texttt{P} \leftarrow \texttt{P} + instruction\_size(\texttt{P});$

## Get instructions

$\boxed{\texttt{get\_variable } \texttt{V}n, \texttt{A}i}$

Place the contents of register A$i$ into variable V$n$. Continue execution with the following instruction.

$\texttt{V}n \leftarrow \texttt{A}i;$
$\texttt{P} \leftarrow \texttt{P} + instruction\_size(\texttt{P});$

$\boxed{\texttt{get\_value } \texttt{V}n, \texttt{A}i}$

Unify variable V$n$ and register A$i$. Backtrack on failure, otherwise continue execution with following instruction.

$unify(\texttt{V}n, \texttt{A}i);$
**if** *fail*
  **then** *backtrack*
  **else** $\texttt{P} \leftarrow \texttt{P} + instruction\_size(\texttt{P});$

> get_structure $f$, A$i$

If the dereferenced value of register A$i$ is an unbound variable, then bind that variable to a new STR cell pointing to $f$ pushed on the heap and set mode to write; otherwise, if it is a STR cell pointing to functor $f$, then set register S to the heap address following that functor cell's and set mode to read. If it is not a STR cell or if the functor is different than $f$, fail. Backtrack on failure, otherwise continue execution with following instruction.

$$addr \leftarrow deref(\text{A}i);$$
**case** STORE $[addr]$ **of**
$\quad \langle \text{REF}, \_ \rangle :$ HEAP$[\text{H}] \leftarrow \langle \text{STR}, \text{H}+1 \rangle;$
$\qquad\qquad\qquad$ HEAP$[\text{H}+1] \leftarrow f;$
$\qquad\qquad\qquad bind(addr, \text{H});$
$\qquad\qquad\qquad \text{H} \leftarrow \text{H}+2;$
$\qquad\qquad\qquad mode \leftarrow \text{write};$
$\quad \langle \text{STR}, a \rangle :$ **if** HEAP$[a] = f$
$\qquad\qquad\qquad$ **then**
$\qquad\qquad\qquad\quad$ **begin**
$\qquad\qquad\qquad\qquad \text{S} \leftarrow a+1;$
$\qquad\qquad\qquad\qquad mode \leftarrow \text{read}$
$\qquad\qquad\qquad\quad$ **end**
$\qquad\qquad\qquad$ **else** $fail \leftarrow$ **true**;
$\quad$ **other** $\quad :$ $fail \leftarrow$ **true**;
**endcase**;
**if** $fail$
$\quad$ **then** $backtrack$
$\quad$ **else** $\text{P} \leftarrow \text{P} + instruction\_size(\text{P});$

---

get_list A$i$

---

If the dereferenced value of register A$i$ is an unbound variable, then bind
that variable to a new LIS cell pushed on the heap and set mode to write;
otherwise, if it is a LIS cell, then set register S to the heap address it contains
and set mode to read. If it is not a LIS cell, fail. Backtrack on failure,
otherwise continue execution with following instruction.

$$addr \leftarrow deref(\text{A}i);$$
**case** STORE [$addr$] **of**
$\quad\langle$ REF , _ $\rangle$ :  HEAP [H] $\leftarrow \langle$ LIS , H $+ 1 \rangle$;
$\qquad\qquad\qquad$ $bind(addr, \text{H})$;
$\qquad\qquad\qquad$ H $\leftarrow$ H $+ 1$;
$\qquad\qquad\qquad$ $mode \leftarrow$ write;
$\quad\langle$ LIS , $a \rangle$ :  S $\leftarrow a$;
$\qquad\qquad\qquad$ $mode \leftarrow$ read;
$\quad$**other** $\qquad$ :  $fail \leftarrow$ **true**;
**endcase**;
**if** $fail$
$\quad$**then** $backtrack$
$\quad$**else** P $\leftarrow$ P $+ instruction\_size(\text{P})$;

---

get_constant $c$, A$i$

---

If the dereferenced value of register A$i$ is an unbound variable, bind that
variable to constant $c$. Otherwise, fail if it is not the constant $c$. Backtrack on
failure, otherwise continue execution with following instruction.

$$addr \leftarrow deref(\text{A}i);$$
**case** STORE [$addr$] **of**
$\quad\langle$ REF , _ $\rangle$ :  STORE [$addr$] $\leftarrow \langle$ CON , $c \rangle$;
$\qquad\qquad\qquad$ $trail(addr)$;
$\quad\langle$ CON , $c' \rangle$ :  $fail \leftarrow (c \neq c')$;
$\quad$**other** $\qquad$ :  $fail \leftarrow$ **true**;
**endcase**;
**if** $fail$
$\quad$**then** $backtrack$
$\quad$**else** P $\leftarrow$ P $+ instruction\_size(\text{P})$;

## Set instructions

### set_variable V$n$

Push a new unbound REF cell onto
the heap and copy it into variable V$n$.
Continue execution with the following
instruction.

HEAP[H] ← ⟨REF, H⟩;
V$n$ ← HEAP[H];
H ← H + 1;
P ← P + *instruction_size*(P);

### set_value V$n$

Push V$n$'s value onto the heap. Continue execution with the following instruction.

HEAP[H] ← V$n$;
H ← H + 1;
P ← P + *instruction_size*(P);

### set_local_value V$n$

If the dereferenced value of V$n$ is an
unbound heap variable, push a copy
of it onto the heap. If the dereferenced value is an unbound stack
address, push a new unbound REF
cell onto the heap and bind the stack
variable to it. Continue execution
with the following instruction.

*addr* ← *deref*(V$n$);
**if** *addr* < H
  **then** HEAP[H] ← HEAP[*addr*]
  **else**
    **begin**
      HEAP[H] ← ⟨REF, H⟩;
      *bind*(*addr*, H)
    **end**;
H ← H + 1;
P ← P + *instruction_size*(P);

### set_constant $c$

Push the constant $c$ onto the heap. Continue execution with the following instruction.

HEAP[H] ← ⟨CON, $c$⟩;
H ← H + 1;
P ← P + *instruction_size*(P);

$\boxed{\texttt{set\_void } n}$

Push $n$ new unbound REF cells onto the heap. Continue execution with the following instruction.

**for** $i \leftarrow$ H **to** H $+ n - 1$ **do**
    HEAP$[i] \leftarrow \langle$ REF $, i \rangle$;
H $\leftarrow$ H $+ n$;
P $\leftarrow$ P $+$ *instruction_size*(P);

## Unify instructions

$\boxed{\texttt{unify\_variable } Vn}$

In read mode, place the contents of heap address S into variable $Vn$; in write mode, push a new unbound REF cell onto the heap and copy it into $Xi$. In either mode, increment S by one. Continue execution with the following instruction.

**case** *mode* **of**
    read  : $Vn \leftarrow$ HEAP$[S]$;
    write: HEAP$[H] \leftarrow \langle$ REF $,$ H $\rangle$;
              $Vn \leftarrow$ HEAP$[H]$;
              H $\leftarrow$ H $+ 1$;
**endcase**;
S $\leftarrow$ S $+ 1$;
P $\leftarrow$ P $+$ *instruction_size*(P);

$\boxed{\texttt{unify\_value } Vn}$

In read mode, unify variable $Vn$ and heap address S; in write mode, push the value of $Vn$ onto the heap. In either mode, increment S by one. Backtrack on failure, otherwise continue execution with following instruction.

**case** *mode* **of**
    read  : *unify*($Vn$, S);
    write: HEAP$[H] \leftarrow Vn$;
              H $\leftarrow$ H $+ 1$;
**endcase**;
S $\leftarrow$ S $+ 1$;
**if** *fail*
    **then** *backtrack*
    **else** P $\leftarrow$ P $+$ *instruction_size*(P);

---
unify_local_value V*n*
---

In read mode, unify variable V*n* and heap address S. In write mode, if the dereferenced value of V*n* is an unbound heap variable, push a copy of it onto the heap. If the dereferenced value is an unbound stack address, push a new unbound REF cell onto the heap and bind the stack variable to it. In either mode, increment S by one. Backtrack on failure, otherwise continue execution with following instruction.

> **case** *mode* **of**
>     read  :  *unify*(V*n*, S);
>     write :  *addr* ← *deref*(V*n*);
>               **if** *addr* < H
>                 **then** HEAP[H] ← HEAP[*addr*]
>               **else**
>                 **begin**
>                   HEAP[H] ← ⟨REF, H⟩;
>                   *bind*(*addr*, H)
>                 **end**;
>               H ← H + 1;
> **endcase**;
> S ← S + 1;
> **if** *fail*
>     **then** *backtrack*
>     **else** P ← P + *instruction_size*(P);

$\boxed{\texttt{unify\_constant } c}$

In `read` mode, dereference the heap address S. If the result is an unbound variable, bind that variable to the constant $c$; otherwise, fail if the result is different than constant $c$. In `write` mode, push the constant $c$ onto the heap. Backtrack on failure, otherwise continue execution with following instruction.

> **case** *mode* **of**
>     read  :  *addr* ← *deref*(S);
>                  **case** STORE [*addr*] **of**
>                     $\langle$ REF , _ $\rangle$  :  STORE [*addr*] ← $\langle$ CON , $c$ $\rangle$;
>                                    *trail*(*addr*);
>                     $\langle$ CON , $c'$ $\rangle$ :  *fail* ← ($c \neq c'$);
>                     **other**     :  *fail* ← **true**;
>                  **endcase**;
>    write:  HEAP [H] ← $\langle$ CON , $c$ $\rangle$;
>                H ← H + 1;
>   **endcase**;
>   **if** *fail*
>     **then** *backtrack*
>     **else** P ← P + *instruction_size*(P);

$\boxed{\texttt{unify\_void } n}$

In `write` mode, push $n$ new unbound REF cells onto the heap. In `read` mode, skip the next $n$ heap cells starting at location S. Continue execution with the following instruction.

> **case** *mode* **of**
>   read  :  S ← S + $n$;
>   write:  **for** $i$ ← H **to** H + $n$ − 1 **do**
>               HEAP [$i$] ← $\langle$ REF , $i$ $\rangle$;
>              H ← H + $n$;
> **endcase**;
> P ← P + *instruction_size*(P);

## Control instructions

| allocate |

Allocate a new environment on the stack, setting its continuation environment and continuation point fields to current $E$ and $CP$, respectively. Continue execution with the following instruction.

> **if** $E > B$
>   **then** $newE \leftarrow E + \text{CODE}[\text{STACK}[E + 1] - 1] + 2$
>   **else** $newE \leftarrow B + \text{STACK}[B] + 8;$
> $\text{STACK}[newE] \leftarrow E;$
> $\text{STACK}[newE + 1] \leftarrow CP;$
> $E \leftarrow newE;$
> $P \leftarrow P + instruction\_size(P);$

| deallocate |

Remove the environment frame at stack location $E$ from the stack by resetting $E$ to the value of its CE field and the continuation pointer $CP$ to the value of its $CP$ field. Continue execution with the following instruction.

$CP \leftarrow \text{STACK}[E + 1];$
$E \leftarrow \text{STACK}[E];$
$P \leftarrow P + instruction\_size(P);$

| call $P, N$ |

If $P$ is defined, then save the current choice point's address in $B0$ and the value of current continuation in $CP$, and continue execution with instruction labeled $P$, with $N$ stack variables remaining in the current environment; otherwise, backtrack.

**if** $defined(P)$
**then**
  **begin**
    $CP \leftarrow P + instruction\_size(P);$
    $num\_of\_args \leftarrow arity(P);$
    $B0 \leftarrow B;$
    $P \leftarrow @(P)$
  **end**
**else** $backtrack;$

---

execute $P$

If $P$ s defined, then save the current choice point's address in B0 and continue execution with instruction labeled $P$; otherwise, backtrack.

**if** *defined*($P$)
   **then**
      **begin**
         *num_of_args* ← *arity*($P$);
         B0 ← B;
         P ← @($P$)
      **end**
   **else** *backtrack*;

---

proceed

Continue execution at instruction whose address is indicated by the continuation register CP.

P ← CP;

## Choice instructions

$\boxed{\texttt{try\_me\_else}\ L}$

Allocate a new choice point frame on the stack setting its next clause field to $L$ and the other fields according to the current context, and set B to point to it. Continue execution with following instruction.

> **if** E > B
>> **then** $newB$ ← E + CODE[STACK[E + 1] − 1] + 2
>> **else** $newB$ ← B + STACK[B] + 8;
>
> STACK[$newB$] ← $num\_of\_args$;
> $n$ ← STACK[$newB$];
> **for** $i$ ← 1 **to** $n$ **do** STACK[$newB + i$] ← A$i$;
> STACK[$newB + n + 1$] ← E;
> STACK[$newB + n + 2$] ← CP;
> STACK[$newB + n + 3$] ← B;
> STACK[$newB + n + 4$] ← $L$;
> STACK[$newB + n + 5$] ← TR;
> STACK[$newB + n + 6$] ← H;
> STACK[$newB + n + 7$] ← B0;
> B ← $newB$;
> HB ← H;
> P ← P + $instruction\_size$(P);

$\boxed{\texttt{retry\_me\_else}\ L}$

Having backtracked to the current choice point, reset all the necessary information from it and update its next clause field to $L$. Continue execution with following instruction.

> $n$ ← STACK[B];
> **for** $i$ ← 1 **to** $n$ **do** A$i$ ← STACK[B + $i$];
> E ← STACK[B + $n$ + 1];
> CP ← STACK[B + $n$ + 2];
> STACK[B + $n$ + 4] ← $L$;
> $unwind\_trail$(STACK[B + $n$ + 5], TR);
> TR ← STACK[B + $n$ + 5];
> H ← STACK[B + $n$ + 6];
> HB ← H;
> P ← P + $instruction\_size$(P);

---

`trust_me`

Having backtracked to the current choice point, reset all the necessary information from it, then discard it by resetting B to its predecessor. Continue execution with following instruction.

$n \leftarrow$ STACK[B];
**for** $i \leftarrow 1$ **to** $n$ **do** A$i \leftarrow$ STACK[B + $i$];
E $\leftarrow$ STACK[B + $n$ + 1];
CP $\leftarrow$ STACK[B + $n$ + 2];
*unwind_trail*(STACK[B + $n$ + 5], TR);
TR $\leftarrow$ STACK[B + $n$ + 5];
H $\leftarrow$ STACK[B + $n$ + 6];
B $\leftarrow$ STACK[B + $n$ + 3];
HB $\leftarrow$ STACK[B + $n$ + 6];
P $\leftarrow$ P + *instruction_size*(P);

---

`try L`

Allocate a new choice point frame on the stack setting its next clause field to the following instruction and the other fields according to the current context, and set B to point to it. Continue execution with instruction labeled $L$.

**if** E > B
**then** *newB* $\leftarrow$ E + CODE[STACK[E + 1] − 1] + 2
**else** *newB* $\leftarrow$ B + STACK[B] + 8;
STACK[*newB*] $\leftarrow$ *num_of_args*;
$n \leftarrow$ STACK[*newB*];
**for** $i \leftarrow 1$ **to** $n$ **do** STACK[*newB* + $i$] $\leftarrow$ A$i$;
STACK[*newB* + $n$ + 1] $\leftarrow$ E;
STACK[*newB* + $n$ + 2] $\leftarrow$ CP;
STACK[*newB* + $n$ + 3] $\leftarrow$ B;
STACK[*newB* + $n$ + 4] $\leftarrow$ P + *instruction_size*(P);
STACK[*newB* + $n$ + 5] $\leftarrow$ TR;
STACK[*newB* + $n$ + 6] $\leftarrow$ H;
STACK[*newB* + $n$ + 7] $\leftarrow$ B0;
B $\leftarrow$ *newB*;
HB $\leftarrow$ H;
P $\leftarrow$ $L$;

$\boxed{\texttt{retry } L}$

Having backtracked to the current choice point, reset all the necessary information from it and update its next clause field to following instruction. Continue execution with instruction labeled $L$.

$n \leftarrow \texttt{STACK[B]};$
**for** $i \leftarrow 0$ **to** $n-1$ **do** A$i \leftarrow \texttt{STACK[B}+i];$
$\texttt{E} \leftarrow \texttt{STACK[B}+n+1];$
$\texttt{CP} \leftarrow \texttt{STACK[B}+n+2];$
$\texttt{STACK[B}+n+4] \leftarrow \texttt{P} + instruction\_size(\texttt{P});$
$unwind\_trail(\texttt{STACK[B}+n+5], \texttt{TR});$
$\texttt{TR} \leftarrow \texttt{STACK[B}+n+5];$
$\texttt{H} \leftarrow \texttt{STACK[B}+n+6];$
$\texttt{HB} \leftarrow \texttt{H};$
$\texttt{P} \leftarrow L;$

$\boxed{\texttt{trust } L}$

Having backtracked to the current choice point, reset all necessary information from it, then discard it by resetting B to its predecessor. Continue execution with instruction labeled $L$.

$n \leftarrow \texttt{STACK[B]};$
**for** $i \leftarrow 1$ **to** $n$ **do** A$i \leftarrow \texttt{STACK[B}+i];$
$\texttt{E} \leftarrow \texttt{STACK[B}+n+1];$
$\texttt{CP} \leftarrow \texttt{STACK[B}+n+2];$
$unwind\_trail(\texttt{STACK[B}+n+5], \texttt{TR});$
$\texttt{TR} \leftarrow \texttt{STACK[B}+n+5];$
$\texttt{H} \leftarrow \texttt{STACK[B}+n+6];$
$\texttt{B} \leftarrow \texttt{STACK[B}+n+3];$
$\texttt{HB} \leftarrow \texttt{STACK[B}+n+6];$
$\texttt{P} \leftarrow L;$

## Indexing instructions

$\boxed{\texttt{switch\_on\_term } V, C, L, S}$

Jump to the instruction labeled, respectively, $V$, $C$, $L$, or $S$, depending on whether the dereferenced value of argument register A1 is a variable, a constant, a non-empty list, or a structure, respectively.

**case** $\texttt{STORE}[deref(\texttt{A1})]$ **of**
  $\langle \texttt{REF}, \_\rangle \,:\, \texttt{P} \leftarrow V;$
  $\langle \texttt{CON}, \_\rangle \,:\, \texttt{P} \leftarrow C;$
  $\langle \texttt{LIS}, \_\rangle \,:\, \texttt{P} \leftarrow L;$
  $\langle \texttt{STR}, \_\rangle \,:\, \texttt{P} \leftarrow S;$
**endcase;**

---

$\boxed{\texttt{switch\_on\_constant } N, T}$

The dereferenced value of regis-   $\langle\, tag\,,\, val\,\rangle \leftarrow \texttt{STORE}\,[deref(\texttt{A1})]\,;$
ter A1 being a constant, jump to   $\langle\, found\,,\, inst\,\rangle \leftarrow get\_hash(val, T, N);$
the instruction associated to it in   **if** *found*
hash-table $T$ of size $N$. If the      **then** P $\leftarrow$ *inst*
constant found in A1 is not one in      **else** *backtrack*;
the table, backtrack.

---

$\boxed{\texttt{switch\_on\_structure } N, T}$

The dereferenced value of regis-   $\langle\, tag\,,\, val\,\rangle \leftarrow \texttt{STORE}\,[deref(\texttt{A1})]\,;$
ter A1 being a structure, jump to   $\langle\, found\,,\, inst\,\rangle \leftarrow get\_hash(val, T, N);$
the instruction associated to it in   **if** *found*
hash-table $T$ of size $N$. If the      **then** P $\leftarrow$ *inst*
functor of the structure found in      **else** *backtrack*;
A1 is not one in the table, back-
track.

## Cut instructions

$\boxed{\texttt{neck\_cut}}$

If there is a choice point after that   **if** B > B0
indicated by B0, discard it and tidy     **then**
the trail up to that point. Continue       **begin**
execution with following instruction.         B $\leftarrow$ B0;
      *tidy_trail*
    **end**;
  P $\leftarrow$ P + *instruction_size*(P);

$\boxed{\texttt{get\_level Y}n}$

Set Y$n$ to the current value of B0.   $\texttt{STACK}\,[\texttt{E}+2+n] \leftarrow \texttt{B0};$
Continue execution with following in-   P $\leftarrow$ P + *instruction_size*(P);
struction.

$\boxed{\text{cut } Yn}$

Discard all (if any) choice points after
that indicated by $Yn$, and tidy the trail
up to that point. Continue execution
with following instruction.

**if** $B > \text{STACK}[E+2+n]$
**then**
  **begin**
    $B \leftarrow \text{STACK}[E+2+n]$;
    *tidy_trail*
  **end**;
$P \leftarrow P + instruction\_size(P)$;

## B.2 WAM ancillary operations

---

**procedure** *backtrack*;
  **begin**
    **if** $B = bottom\_of\_stack$
    **then** *fail_and_exit_program*
    **else**
      **begin**
        $B0 \leftarrow \text{STACK}[B + \text{STACK}[B] + 7]$;
        $P \leftarrow \text{STACK}[B + \text{STACK}[B] + 4]$
      **end**
  **end** *backtrack*;

---

The *backtrack* **operation**

---

**function** *deref*(*a* : *address*) : *address*;
  **begin**
    $\langle\, tag\, ,\, value\, \rangle \leftarrow$ STORE $[\,a\,]$;
    **if** ($tag$ = REF) $\wedge$ ($value \neq a$)
      **then return** *deref*($value$)
      **else return** $a$
  **end** *deref*;

---

**The *deref* operation**

---

**procedure** *bind*($a_1, a_2$ : *address*);
  $\langle\, t_1\, ,\, {}_- \rangle \leftarrow$ STORE $[\,a_1\,]$; $\langle\, t_2\, ,\, {}_- \rangle \leftarrow$ STORE $[\,a_2\,]$;
  **if** ($t_1$ = REF) $\wedge$ (($t_2 \neq$ REF) $\vee$ ($a_2 < a_1$))
    **then**
      **begin**
        STORE $[\,a_1\,] \leftarrow$ STORE $[\,a_2\,]$; *trail*($a_1$)
      **end**
    **else**
      **begin**
        STORE $[\,a_2\,] \leftarrow$ STORE $[\,a_1\,]$; *trail*($a_2$)
      **end**
  **end** *bind*;

---

**The *bind* operation**

---

**procedure** *trail*($a$ : *address*);
  **if** ($a <$ HB) $\lor$ ((H $< a$) $\land$ ($a <$ B))
    **then**
      **begin**
        TRAIL[TR] $\leftarrow a$;
        TR $\leftarrow$ TR + 1
      **end**
**end** *trail*;

---

The *trail* **operation**

---

**procedure** *unwind_trail*($a_1, a_2$ : *address*);
  **for** $i \leftarrow a_1$ **to** $a_2 - 1$ **do**
    STORE[TRAIL[$i$]] $\leftarrow \langle$ REF , TRAIL[$i$] $\rangle$;
**end** *unwind_trail*;

---

The *unwind_trail* **operation**

---

**procedure** *tidy_trail*;
  $i \leftarrow$ STACK[B + STACK[B] + 5];
  **while** $i <$ TR **do**
    **if** (TRAIL[$i$] $<$ HB) $\lor$ ((H $<$ TRAIL[$i$]) $\land$ (TRAIL[$i$] $<$ B))
      **then** $i \leftarrow i + 1$
      **else**
        **begin**
          TRAIL[$i$] $\leftarrow$ TRAIL[TR $-$ 1];
          TR $\leftarrow$ TR $-$ 1
        **end**
**end** *tidy_trail*;

---

The *tidy_trail* **operation**

```
procedure unify(a₁, a₂ : address);
  push(a₁, PDL); push(a₂, PDL);
  fail ← false;
  while ¬(empty(PDL) ∨ fail) do
    begin
      d₁ ← deref(pop(PDL)); d₂ ← deref(pop(PDL));
      if d₁ ≠ d₂ then
        begin
          ⟨t₁, v₁⟩ ← STORE[d₁]; ⟨t₂, v₂⟩ ← STORE[d₂];
          if t₁ = REF then bind(d₁, d₂)
            else
              case t₂ of
                REF : bind(d₁, d₂);
                CON : fail ← (t₁ ≠ CON) ∨ (v₁ ≠ v₂);
                LIS : if t₁ ≠ LIS then fail ← true
                        else
                          begin
                            push(v₁, PDL); push(v₂, PDL);
                            push(v₁ + 1, PDL); push(v₂ + 1, PDL)
                          end;
                STR : if t₁ ≠ STR then fail ← true
                        else
                          begin
                            f₁/n₁ ← STORE[v₁]; f₂/n₂ ← STORE[v₂];
                            if (f₁ ≠ f₂) ∨ (n₁ ≠ n₂) then fail ← true
                              else
                                for i ← 1 to n₁ do
                                  begin
                                    push(v₁ + i, PDL); push(v₂ + i, PDL)
                                  end
                          end
              endcase
        end
    end
end unify;
```

**The complete *unify* operation**

## B.3 WAM memory layout and registers

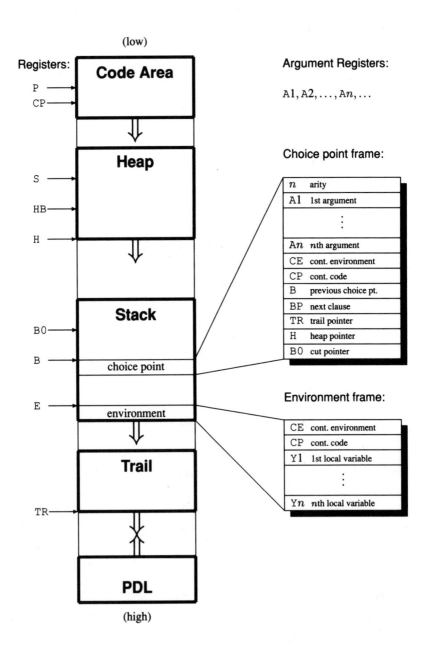

# References

[AHU74]     Alfred Aho, John Hopcroft, and Jeffrey Ullmann. *The Design and Analysis of Computer Algorithms*. Addison-Wesley, Reading, MA, 1974.

[AK90]     Hassan Aït-Kaci. The WAM: a (real) tutorial. PRL Research Report Number 5, Digital Equipment Corporation, Paris Research Laboratory, Rueil-Malmaison, France, 1990.

[Boi88]     Patrice Boizumault. *Prolog: l'implantation*. Etudes et recherches en informatique. Masson, Paris, France, 1988.

[BP84]     Maurice Bruynooghe and Luis M. Pereira. Deduction revision by intelligent backtracking. In John A. Campbell, editor, *Implementations of Prolog*, pages 194–215. Ellis Horwood, Ltd., Chichester, UK, 1984.

[CCF88]     Christian Codognet, Philippe Codognet, and Gilberto Filè. Yet another intelligent backtracking method. In Robert Kowalski and Kenneth Bowen, editors, *Logic Programming: Proceedings of the Fifth International Conference and Symposium*, pages 447–465, Cambridge, MA, 1988. MIT Press.

[Chu90]     Damian Chu. Private communicatiion. Electronic Mail, August 1990.

[CM84]     William F. Clocksin and Christopher S. Mellish. *Programming in Prolog*. Springer-Verlag, Berlin, Germany, 2nd edition, 1984.

[Cox84]     Peter T. Cox. Finding backtrack points for intelligent backtracking. In John A. Campbell, editor, *Implementations of Prolog*, pages 216–133. Ellis Horwood, Ltd., Chichester, UK, 1984.

[Deb86]     Saumya K. Debray. Register allocation in a Prolog machine. In *Proceedings of the Symposium on Logic Programming*, pages 267–275. IEEE Computer Society, September 1986.

[Deb89]     Saumya K. Debray. Static inference of modes and data dependencies in logic programs. *ACM Transactions on Programming Languages and Systems*, 11(3):418–450, July 1989.

[DW86a]     Saumya K. Debray and David S. Warren. Automatic mode inference for Prolog programs. In *Proceedings of the Symposium on Logic Programming*, pages 78–88. IEEE Computer Society, September 1986.

[DW86b]     Saumya K. Debray and David S. Warren. Detection and optimization of functional computations in Prolog. In Ehud Shapiro, editor, *Proceedings of the Third International Conference on Logic Programming*, Berlin, Germany, 1986. Springer-Verlag. Lecture Notes in Computer Science 225.

[DW89]     Saumya K. Debray and David S. Warren. Functional computations in logic programs. *ACM Transactions on Programming Languages and Systems*, 11(3):451–481, July 1989.

[GLLO85]  John Gabriel, Tim Lindholm, Ewing Lusk, and Ross Overbeek. A tutorial on the
          Warren abstract machine. Privately circulated draft, Argonne National Laboratory,
          Mathematics and Computer Science Division, Argonne, IL 60439., 1985.

[Han90]   Michael Hanus. Private communication. Technical correspondence, December 1990.

[Her71]   Jacques Herbrand. *Logical Writings*. Harvard University Press, Cambridge, MA,
          1971. Edited by Warren D. Goldfarb.

[JDM88]   Gerda Janssens, Bart Demoen, and Andre Mariën. Improving the register allocation
          in WAM by reordering unification. In Robert Kowalski and Kenneth Bowen,
          editors, *Logic Programming: Proceedings of the Fifth International Conference and
          Symposium*, pages 1388–1402, Cambridge, MA, 1988. MIT Press.

[Kow79]   Robert A. Kowalski. *Logic for Problem Solving*, volume 7 of *Artificial Intelligence
          Series*. North Holland, New York, NY, 1979.

[Kur87]   Peter Kursawe. How to invent a Prolog machine. *New Generation Computing*,
          5:97–114, 1987.

[Mel85]   Christopher S. Mellish. Some global optimizations for a Prolog compiler. *Journal of
          Logic Programming*, 1:143–166, 1985.

[MM82]    Alberto Martelli and Ugo Montanari. An efficient unification algorithm. *ACM
          Transactions on Programming Languages and Systems*, 4(2):258–282, April 1982.

[MW88]    David Maier and David S. Warren. *Computing with Logic: Logic Programming with
          Prolog*. Benjamin/Cummings, Menlo Park, CA, 1988.

[Per90]   Fernando Pereira. Personal communication. Electronic mail, April 1990.

[PP82]    Luis M. Pereira and Antonio Porto. Selective backtracking. In Keith L. Clark and
          Sten-Åke Tärnlund, editors, *Logic Programming*, pages 107–114. Academic Press,
          New York, NY, 1982.

[Rob65]   John A. Robinson. A machine-oriented logic based on the resolution principle.
          *Journal of the ACM*, 12:23–41, January 1965.

[Ros91]   Dean Rosenzweig. Personal communication. Electronic mail, March 1991.

[Rus89]   David M. Russinoff. A verified Prolog compiler for the Warren abstract machine.
          MCC Technical Report Number ACT-ST-292-89, Microelectronics and Computer
          Technology Corporation, Austin, TX, July 1989.

[vH90]    Pascal van Hentenryck. Private communication. Electronic mail, September 1990.

[vR90]    Peter L. van Roy. *Can Logic Programming Execute as Fast as Imperative Program-
          ming?* PhD thesis, University of California at Berkeley, Berkeley, CA, December
          1990.

[vRD90]    Peter L. van Roy and Alvin Despain. The benefits of global dataflow analysis for an optimizing Prolog compiler. In Saumya Debray and Manuel Hermenegildo, editors, *Logic Programming: Proceedings of the 1990 North American Conference*, pages 491–515, Cambridge, MA, 1990. MIT Press.

[War83]    David H. D. Warren. An abstract Prolog instruction set. Technical Note 309, SRI International, Menlo Park, CA, October 1983.

[War88]    David H. D. Warren. Implementation of Prolog. Lecture notes, Tutorial No. 3, 5th International Conference and Symposium on Logic Programming, Seattle, WA, August 1988.

[War89]    David H. D. Warren. Private communication. Electronic mail, October 1989.

[War90]    David H. D. Warren. Private communication. Electronic mail, September 1990.

[Zho90]    Neng-Fa Zhou. *Backtracking Optimizations in Compiled Prolog*. PhD thesis, Kyushu University, Fukuoka, Japan, November 1990.

[ZTU90]    Neng-Fa Zhou, T. Takagi, and K. Ushijima. A matching tree oriented abstract machine for prolog. In David H. D. Warren and Peter Szeredi, editors, *Logic Programming: Proceedings of the Seventh International Conference*, pages 159–173, Cambridge, MA, 1990. MIT Press.

# Index

The MIT Press, with Peter Denning as general consulting editor, publishes computer science books in the following series:

**ACL-MIT Press Series in Natural Language Processing**
Aravind K. Joshi, Mark Liberman, and Karen Sparck Jones, editors

**ACM Doctoral Dissertation Award and Distinguished Dissertation Series**

**Artificial Intelligence**
Patrick Winston, founding editor
J. Michael Brady, Daniel G. Bobrow, and Randall Davis, editors

**Charles Babbage Institute Reprint Series for the History of Computing**
Martin Campbell-Kelly, editor

**Computer Systems**
Herb Schwetman, editor

**Explorations with Logo**
E. Paul Goldenberg, editor

**Foundations of Computing**
Michael Garey and Albert Meyer, editors

**History of Computing**
I. Bernard Cohen and William Aspray, editors

**Logic Programming**
Ehud Shapiro, editor; Fernando Pereira, Koichi Furukawa, Jean-Louis Lassez, and David H. D. Warren, associate editors

**The MIT Press Electrical Engineering and Computer Science Series**

**Research Monographs in Parallel and Distributed Processing**
Christopher Jesshope and David Klappholz, editors

**Scientific and Engineering Computation**
Janusz Kowalik, editor

**Technical Communication and Information Systems**
Ed Barrett, editor